PEPPER
CLOVES
GINGER
CAKE
CHEST

Southern Living

The SOUTHERN HERITAGE COOKBOOK LIBRARY

Ardenter
TRADE MARK
Mustard

Molly says it has no equal
CHAS COUNSELMAN & CO'S.
ROYAL HAMS.

The SOUTHERN HERITAGE All Pork COOKBOOK

OXMOOR HOUSE
Birmingham, Alabama

Southern Living.

The Southern Heritage Cookbook Library

Book Division of Southern Progress Corporation
P.O. Box 2262, Birmingham, Alabama 35201

Library of Congress Catalog Number: 84-60634
ISBN: 0-8487-0611-0

Manufactured in the United States of America

The Southern Heritage ALL PORK Cookbook

Manager, Editorial Projects: Ann H. Harvey
Southern Living® *Foods Editor*: Jean W. Liles
Production Editor: Joan E. Denman
Foods Editor: Katherine M. Eakin
Director, Test Kitchen: Laura N. Nestelroad
Test Kitchen Home Economists: Pattie B. Booker, Kay E. Clarke, Elizabeth J. Taliaferro, Dee Waller
Production Manager: Jerry R. Higdon
Copy Editor: Melinda E. West
Editorial Assistants: Patty E. Howdon, Mary Ann Laurens, Karen P. Traccarella
Food Photographer: Jim Bathie
Food Stylist: Sara Jane Ball
Layout Designer: Christian von Rosenvinge
Mechanical Artist: Faith Nance
Research Editors: Evelyn deFrees, Alicia Hathaway

Special Consultants

Art Director: Irwin Glusker
Heritage Consultant: Meryle Evans
Foods Writer: Lillian B. Marshall
Food and Recipe Consultants: Marilyn Wyrick Ingram, Audrey P. Stehle

Cover (clockwise from top): Sykes Inn Smithfield Ham (page 66), Deep South Oven-Barbecued Ribs (page 33), Baked Stuffed Pork Chops (page 26), and Savory Ham-Veal Ring (page 87). Photograph by George Ratkai.

Abby Aldrich Rockefeller Folk Art Center, Williamsburg, Virginia

CONTENTS

An assortment of smoked meats which have been home cured in a smokehouse in Jasper, Alabama.

INTRODUCTION

From its disputed origin in hither Asia or alpine Europe, pork began to be domesticated and its succulent meat devoured by every succeeding civilization, with the exception of some Middle-Eastern cultures. Hebrews and Egyptians considered pork meat impure although, oddly, Egyptians annually sacrificed pigs to Osiris and ate the meat. In parts of the ancient world, pork was thought to cause leprosy. Classic mythology drew liberally on the pig. It was the symbol of Demeter, for example, goddess of corn. Corn, pigs, and humans have been bound together interdependently for these thousands of years.

Corn, the old generic term for grain, was the name given to Indian maize by the colonists; to them it was another form of barley, rye, or wheat. They quickly learned it was more important than all the rest, at least to them.

Pork appeared in politics long before the "pork barrel" was invented for use in accusatory speeches: Patrick Henry once said that Thomas Jefferson had become so "Frenchified that he abjured his native victuals." But political rhetoric, too, is native to the South, and a glance at Jefferson's recorded menus and inventories shows the inaccuracy of Henry's remark. The meat at Monticello leaned as heavily to pork as at any other rich plantation. The Carters on the James River, for example, assisted by an army of guests and servants, consumed 27,000 pounds of pork a year. The people liked not only hams and bacon, but pig's feet, head cheese, sausage, and more.

It will be recalled that there had been three unsuccessful attempts at colonization by the English on the East Coast prior to the arrival of Captain John Smith's group on the Virginia shore in 1607. All three had vanished without a trace. While they were still trying to adjust, Smith had to return to England because of illness. The remaining settlers, unable to feed their stock, turned pigs, cattle, and horses out to fend for themselves. But the Indians had acquired a taste for beef and pork, and it became increasingly hard for the settlers to find their meat animals. Horses were the epitome of uselessness; they had no loads to carry, nowhere to go. They were to turn up years later as wild herds, affording great sport to the young Tidewater gentry who caught and broke them.

The winter of 1609-1610 stands out in the South's history as "The Starving Time." Smith had been a strict disciplinarian; the people, most of whom considered themselves above laboring, simply gave up. Lord De La Warr, arriving in May, 1610, found a few emaciated human survivors. Appalled, he reported to the Virginia Company that all five or six hundred hogs had been killed, even brood sows. Hens, horses, and mares alike had been killed and eaten. After three years in their new land, the settlers were on the verge of extinction. Stern measures were not long in coming, in the person of Governor Thomas Dale. He arrived in May, 1611, with new breeding stock and a new work ethic. The wan survivors, jarred from their lethargy, were put to work building, clearing, and cultivating.

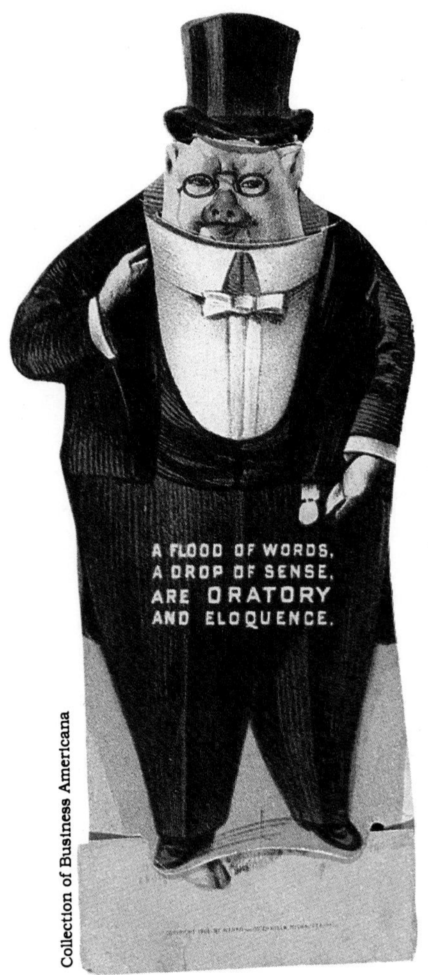

Collection of Business Americana

When Captain Smith returned in 1629, he found about 5,000 industrious people taking care of crops and stock. One of their ploys to guard their hogs from marauding Indians had been to isolate the beasts on an island in the James River. It was a brilliant idea, but overpopulation finally drove some of the porkers of Hog Island to swim for shore.

"How far can a hog swim?" A burning question, surely. Thin hogs can do olympic laps, while fat ones cut their throats with their hooves when they try for the distance. The thin hogs made it to shore, took to the woods, and became famous as the razorbacks which, according to most authorities, are the ancestors of the lean hogs we use for cured hams and bacon. In fall, they battened on the fruits of beech, oak, hickory, chestnut, and persimmon — foods lumped together under the term "mast." The Greeks had used the same method for fattening swine.

With the advent of peanuts, mast acquired a new dimension; hogs were turned into the harvested fields to clean up nuts and roots. It is known that mast-fed pork fat melts at ten degrees lower temperature than that of grain-fed animals and is considered by connoisseurs to produce superior cured meats.

Salt-cured meats had been commonplace for centuries before the colonization of America, but finishing the cure with smoke was a lesson learned from the Indians. The salt the settlers made by evaporating sea water was inferior, so they imported salt from England. Building on African peanuts and Indian wood smoke, Virginia emerged as the hub of a fully fledged pork industry, with Smithfield as its busy capital city. Droves of hogs came in from the newer colonies of the Carolinas and Georgia to be slaughtered, cured, and exported. Pork, closely followed by tobacco, became the leading edge of the Southern colonies' various exports, opening trade with the North, the West Indies, and Europe.

Queen Victoria kept her palace supplied with Virginia hams. Prince Albert, who was German, may have preferred his native Westphalian hams, but history seems mute on the point. What is certain is that the peanut mast, controlled smoke, humidity, and aging came together most amiably in the Smithfield ham, with its finely textured, yellow fat.

Collection of Business Americana

The Southerner's affection for pork has been derided by writers who seem not to like the odor of pork frying. Southern writers, on the other hand, can bring tears with a description of pork's fragrance in the skillet and the preparation of cornbread or biscuits being made to accompany it. The reason for such disparity in the perception of pork is that a Southerner rarely forgets where his loyalties lie. Pork has been the mainstay of his diet, while proving to be the most efficient meat animal known. In three months, three weeks, and three days, a sow can produce a litter of eight pigs. They will put on twice as much weight per pound of feed consumed than will other meat animals and will eat material other beasts will not touch. At the end, a hog will dress out to about 75 percent edible meat, as opposed to 55-60 percent for beef.

Americans, including George Washington and other rich planters, began early to practice selective breeding, aiming for the lean, rangy animal prized for its excellent ham and "streak of fat — streak of lean" bacon. The Spanish, by contrast, brought with them and continued to prefer sleek, fat pork. Cortez's retinue, as he crossed Honduras, included as vanguard a large herd of rounded porkers — lard on the hoof.

Even the leanest of the lean provided some fat for the shortening of the day — lard. Once of utmost importance and now somewhat fallen into disuse, lard can still be found occasionally simmering in a huge black pot behind the farmhouse. And the crisp cracklings are as valuable as ever as a cornbread addition.

Lard is only one of the good things remaining after the hams and bacon are removed. We intend to make sausages from "country" to kielbasa and to cook pork from *barbe-a-queue* which means from beard to tail.

LIVING HIGH ON THE HOG

When the English arrived on the East Coast, the Indians' only domestic animal was the dog. That is not to say, however, that there was no pork to be had. The early Carolinians bartered for pork with the Indians, who hunted the wild descendants of hogs brought to Florida by de Soto before 1550. These ill-tempered beasts had spread northward in search of forage; Florida's natural produce never appealed to them.

By 1700 the average Virginia family would own four or five pigs in addition to chickens and perhaps even a few head of sheep and beef. What this meant was enough surplus to thrust the South's cured and pickled pork into world commerce. Trading ships put in, unloaded, and took on pork.

The yeoman farmer could now choose to market some of his hams and bacon, while keeping back some pork for family use. Eating "high on the hog" was, for him, by no means an everyday affair, but when the occasion warranted, a pork roast could be cooked, or even a suckling pig.

The definitive performance of high-on-the-hog eating took place around the polished mahogany tables of the wealthy, trend-setting households of the Tidewater region. A spit-roasted pig at one end of the board was balanced at the other end with a roast goose; a leg of pork with a roast of beef or lamb. At their three or four o'clock dinners, the fashionable folk covered every inch of their tables with food, matching dishes corner for corner, side for side. Two courses and two tablecloths were the rule, and after the second cloth was removed, nuts, apples, and raisins were served, and toasts offered. President Washington, known for his reticence during dinner, came to life when the cloths were cleared and the wine brought in.

The gentry, of course, enjoyed more of the best cuts of pork more often than did the poor. But rich and poor alike knew the joys of eating pigs' trotters, souse, salt pork, and sausage. Pork was, and is, the South's staple, preferred over beef and right up there with chicken. Roasts are here, and tenderloin, and chops and steaks; feastworthy cuts from high on the Southern hog.

Roast Suckling Pig is the star at a Victorian feast photographed in the dining room of the John Wright Stanly House. Built in the 1780s by the Revolutionary War patriot, the house has been restored as part of the Tryon Palace Complex, New Bern, North Carolina.

VICTORIAN FEAST

Historic symbol of opulence, the roast suckling pig has been proudly served at great feasts from Roman orgies to presidential soirées. Southerners have kept a tradition of roasting a four- to six-week-old pig for their most gala occasions. Nineteenth-century cookbook writers differed upon the positioning of the pig for roasting; kneeling with all legs underneath, or front legs extended? Into the mouth might go an apple, orange, or small ear of corn. In Marion Harland's presentation, the pig knelt on a bed of parsley and celery leaves, was garlanded about the neck with the same, and his mouth held a tuft of white cauliflower. We opted for the apple in our Victorian Feast, recreated at the Tryon Palace Complex in North Carolina.

OYSTERS ON THE HALF SHELL
ROAST SUCKLING PIG
ONION-BREAD DRESSING
RICH BROWN GRAVY
STEAMED WINTER VEGETABLES
SPICED RED APPLES
LEMON CHARLOTTE RUSSE
LEMON CHESS TARTS

Serves 10 to 12

ROAST SUCKLING PIG

1 (14- to 19-pound) suckling pig
1 small red apple
2 seedless grapes

Scrub pig with a stiff brush; rinse cavity, and pat dry. Stuff with aluminum foil. Close cavity with skewers and string, lacing tightly. Truss by bringing feet forward and tying in kneeling position with string. Place a firm ball of aluminum foil in pig's mouth; cover nose, ears, and tail with aluminum foil. Insert meat thermometer in thigh muscle; do not touch bone.

Place pig in a shallow roasting pan. Bake at 325° for 3½ to 4 hours or until meat thermometer registers 170°, basting occasionally with pan drippings.

Transfer pig to a serving platter; reserve 3 tablespoons drippings for gravy. Remove foil from mouth; insert apple. Place grapes in eye sockets. Remove foil from nose, ears, and tail.

To serve, carve along spine, breaking backbone. Yield: 10 to 12 servings.

Virginia Historical Society

Photographer: Jim Bathie

Above: *North entrance of restored Tryon Palace, New Bern, North Carolina.* Left: *1907 feast held to celebrate Jamestown's 300th anniversary year.*

ONION-BREAD DRESSING

2 large onions, chopped
2 cups chopped celery
½ cup butter or margarine
2 cups chicken broth
2 teaspoons salt
½ teaspoon pepper
½ teaspoon rubbed sage
3 eggs, well beaten
2 quarts soft breadcrumbs
3 quarts cornbread crumbs

Sauté onion and celery in butter until tender. Set aside.

Combine chicken broth, salt, pepper, and sage in a large mixing bowl; mix well. Add sautéed vegetables, eggs, and breadcrumbs; stir well.

Spoon dressing into a greased 3½-quart shallow baking dish. Bake at 350° for 45 minutes or until lightly browned. Yield: 10 to 12 servings.

The Maude Moore Latham Memorial Garden at Tryon Palace.

RICH BROWN GRAVY

3 tablespoons pan drippings from roast suckling pig
3 tablespoons all-purpose flour
2 cups beef broth
¼ teaspoon pepper

Heat drippings in a heavy skillet over medium heat. Add flour; stir until smooth. Cook over low heat 2 minutes, stirring constantly. Add beef broth; cook over medium-high heat 2 minutes, stirring constantly, until thickened. Stir in pepper. Serve hot with Onion-Bread Dressing. Yield: 1½ cups.

STEAMED WINTER VEGETABLES

½ cup butter or margarine
1 (2-pound) rutabaga, peeled and sliced
2 medium turnips, peeled and sliced
6 medium carrots, scraped and sliced into thin strips
2 pounds fresh broccoli, cleaned and coarsely chopped
Salt and pepper to taste
Melted butter or margarine

Melt ½ cup butter in a Dutch oven over medium heat. Arrange layers of rutabaga, turnips, and carrots over butter. Place two sheets of waxed paper on top of vegetables; cover with lid. Cook over high heat until steam begins to escape. Reduce heat to low, and cook 20 minutes without removing lid.

Add broccoli; cover and cook 20 minutes over medium heat or until broccoli is tender. Place vegetables in a serving dish. Add salt and pepper to taste. Pour butter over vegetables. Yield: 10 to 12 servings.

SPICED RED APPLES

8 cups sugar
8 cups water
Grated rind of 4 lemons
2 teaspoons red food coloring
32 whole cloves
12 small apples, cored and peeled

Combine sugar and water in a large Dutch oven. Cook over medium heat until sugar dissolves; add lemon rind, food coloring, and cloves. Cook an additional minute. Strain mixture; discard rind and cloves. Add apples; cook, uncovered, 30 minutes or until apples are tender and translucent red in color. Serve hot or chilled with cooking syrup. Yield: 12 apples.

LEMON CHARLOTTE RUSSE

1 envelope unflavored gelatin
1½ cups sugar, divided
4 eggs, separated
½ cup lemon juice
⅛ teaspoon salt
3 tablespoons butter or margarine
1½ teaspoons grated lemon rind
1 teaspoon vanilla extract
14 ladyfingers, split in half lengthwise
1 cup whipping cream, whipped
Sweetened whipped cream

Combine gelatin and 1 cup sugar in top of a double boiler; mix well. Stir in egg yolks, lemon juice, and salt. Cook over boiling water, stirring constantly, 10 minutes or until thickened. Add butter, lemon rind, and vanilla, stirring until butter melts. Chill mixture until partially thickened.

Arrange ladyfingers around bottom and sides of a 9-inch springform pan; set aside.

Beat egg whites (at room temperature) until soft peaks form. Gradually add remaining sugar, 1 tablespoon at a time; beat until stiff peaks form. Fold egg whites and whipped cream into gelatin mixture. Spoon into pan. Cover; chill 4 hours.

To serve, remove sides of springform pan. Garnish with sweetened whipped cream. Yield: 12 servings.

LEMON CHESS TARTS

1½ cups sugar
3 eggs, beaten
3 tablespoons butter or margarine, melted
1½ tablespoons lemon rind
1½ tablespoons lemon juice
¼ teaspoon salt
15 (2¾-inch) tart shells, unbaked

Combine first 6 ingredients; mix well. Spoon mixture into tart shells. Bake at 350° for 35 minutes or until lightly browned. Yield: 15 tarts.

The visitor to Tryon Palace is first struck by its perfect symmetry, whether viewed from the Latham gardens in warm weather or from the interior authentically decked out for an eighteenth-century Christmas. The palace complex, built for Royal Governor William Tryon in 1769 by architect John Hawkes, had suffered through the Revolutionary War, then neglect and vandalism. Finally a disastrous fire in 1798 ended its existence. The painstaking reconstruction, largely financed by Mrs. James Latham and her daughter, Mrs. John Kellenberger, was completed in 1959, a stunning monument to the South's colonial past.

Lemon Chess Tarts and Lemon Charlotte Russe.

Photographer: Jim Bathie

STUFFED ROAST SUCKLING PIG

1 (17- to 20-pound) whole suckling pig
2 teaspoons salt
½ teaspoon rubbed sage
2 pounds mild bulk pork sausage, crumbled
2 large onions, chopped
2 cloves garlic, minced
5 cups soft bread cubes
3 cups raisin bread cubes
2 medium-size cooking apples, unpeeled, cored, and chopped
1 cup chopped walnuts
1 tablespoon salt
2 teaspoons pepper
1 teaspoon dried whole thyme
1 teaspoon ground marjoram
5 eggs, beaten
¾ cup apple cider, divided
½ cup butter or margarine, melted
Fresh parsley sprigs
Spiced crab apples
1 large apple
2 red maraschino cherries

Have butcher dress pig, leaving head, tail, and feet intact. Wash pig thoroughly, and pat dry. Combine 2 teaspoons salt and sage; rub body cavity with mixture. Set aside.

Combine crumbled sausage, onion, and garlic in a very large skillet; sauté until sausage is browned and onion is tender. Remove from heat, and drain well. Stir in bread cubes, chopped apple, walnuts, 1 tablespoon salt, pepper, thyme, and marjoram. Combine eggs and ¼ cup apple cider; mix well, and add to sausage mixture.

Stuff mixture lightly into body cavity of pig; sew opening together securely using heavy string. Place a small block of wood in pig's mouth to prop jaws open. Insert meat thermometer into pig, being careful not to touch fat or bone. Transfer whole pig to a large roasting pan. Combine melted butter and remaining apple cider; mix well, and set aside.

Bake stuffed pig at 350° for 2 hours and 15 minutes or until meat thermometer registers 170°, basting frequently with apple cider mixture.

To serve, transfer stuffing from pig to a serving dish. Transfer whole pig to a large serving platter; garnish platter with parsley sprigs and spiced crab apples. Remove wood block from pig's mouth, and insert apple between jaws. Place maraschino cherries in eye sockets. Cut off legs; carve pork along spine, cracking backbone. Yield: 10 to 15 servings.

Courtesy of The Biltmore House

Electric rotisserie at The Biltmore House, North Carolina.

MARINATED PORK ROAST

½ cup soy sauce
½ cup dry sherry
1 tablespoon dry mustard
1 teaspoon ground ginger
1 teaspoon dried whole thyme
2 cloves garlic, minced
1 (3- to 4-pound) pork loin roast, boned, rolled, and tied
Onion chrysanthemum (optional)
Cherry tomato flowers (optional)
Large bay leaves (optional)

Combine soy sauce, sherry, mustard, ginger, thyme, and garlic in a shallow dish; stir well. Place roast in dish. Cover and marinate roast overnight in refrigerator; turn occasionally.

Remove roast to a well-greased rack in a shallow roasting pan, reserving marinade. Insert meat thermometer, at an angle, into thickest part of roast.

Bake, uncovered, at 325° for 2 hours and 45 minutes or until meat thermometer registers 170°. Baste with reserved marinade every 15 minutes during last 45 minutes of cooking time.

Remove roast to a serving platter. Garnish platter with onion chrysanthemum, cherry tomato flowers, and bay leaves, if desired. Let roast stand 10 to 15 minutes before slicing. Yield: 12 servings.

Cornbread, hominy, and pork comprised the staple diet of the antebellum North Carolinian, as it did that of the majority of Southerners: The "gentry" never comprised more than a small percent of the population. Some considered North Carolina pork "fed on peaches, maize, and such other natural produce" to be "some of the sweetest meat that the world affords."

Marinated Pork Roast, made from boneless loin, with a faintly Oriental air.

ROAST LOIN OF PORK

3 tablespoons soft breadcrumbs
1 small onion, chopped
½ teaspoon salt
½ teaspoon pepper
½ teaspoon rubbed sage
1 tablespoon butter or margarine, melted
1 (3- to 4-pound) pork loin center-cut rib roast, with chine bone removed
1 tablespoon vegetable oil
2 tablespoons all-purpose flour
1 cup water
1 teaspoon salt
⅛ teaspoon pepper

Combine first 6 ingredients in a small mixing bowl; mix well.

Cut 3-inch slits between each chop; stuff mixture into openings. Place roast, fat side up, on a cutting board; score fat in a diamond design. Place roast, fat side up, in a shallow roasting pan. Brush roast with vegetable oil. Insert meat thermometer, being careful not to touch bone or fat. Bake roast, uncovered, at 350° for 1 hour and 45 minutes or until meat thermometer registers 170°.

Remove roast to a warm serving platter; reserve 2 tablespoons pan drippings. Combine drippings and flour in a small saucepan; add water, salt, and pepper, stirring well. Cook, stirring constantly, until thickened and bubbly. Serve gravy with roast. Yield: 6 to 8 servings.

ROAST LOIN OF PORK WITH VEGETABLES

1 teaspoon dried whole rosemary, crushed
1 teaspoon salt
½ teaspoon coarsely ground black pepper
1 (3-pound) pork loin center-cut rib roast, with chine bone notched at each rib
3 medium onions, chopped
2 large carrots, coarsely chopped
4 sprigs fresh parsley
1 bay leaf
2 onions, thinly sliced
2 tablespoons butter or margarine
6 medium-size baking potatoes, peeled and sliced
½ teaspoon salt
¼ teaspoon pepper
2 cups chicken broth, divided
1 tablespoon chopped fresh parsley

Combine rosemary, 1 teaspoon salt, and coarsely ground pepper; sprinkle over entire surface of roast. Place roast, fat side up, in a roasting pan with a cover. Insert meat thermometer, being careful not to touch bone or fat. Bake, uncovered, at 475° for 20 minutes. Place chopped onion, carrots, parsley sprigs, and bay leaf around meat. Reduce heat to 375°; cover and bake an additional 40 minutes.

Sauté sliced onion in butter in a heavy skillet until tender. Set aside.

Place potatoes in a lightly greased 13- x 9- x 2-inch baking dish. Sprinkle with ½ teaspoon salt and ¼ teaspoon pepper. Top with sautéed onion. Pour ½ cup chicken broth over onion and potatoes. Set aside.

Remove roast from roasting pan, reserving vegetable mixture in pan. Place roast in baking dish over onion and potatoes. Bake, uncovered, at 375° on lower oven rack for 45 minutes or until meat thermometer registers 170°.

Add remaining chicken broth to vegetable mixture in roasting pan. Bring to a boil, and cook 5 minutes, stirring frequently. Strain through a sieve into a bowl; discard vegetables. Let broth stand 30 minutes; skim off fat.

Transfer roast, onion, and potatoes to a serving platter. Pour broth over roast. Sprinkle potatoes with chopped parsley. Yield: 6 servings.

OZARK PORK ROAST

¾ teaspoon salt, divided
½ teaspoon pepper, divided
1 (2- to 2½-pound) pork loin end roast
¼ cup all-purpose flour
¼ cup butter or margarine, melted
2 tablespoons vegetable oil
1 medium onion, chopped
4 carrots, cut into 1-inch pieces
4 medium potatoes, peeled and halved

Rub ½ teaspoon salt and ¼ teaspoon pepper over surface of roast; dredge roast in flour. Brown roast on all sides in butter and oil in a large, deep cast-iron skillet.

Remove roast from skillet; drain on paper towels. Sauté onion in pan drippings until tender. Place roast over onions; add carrots and potatoes. Sprinkle remaining salt and pepper over vegetables.

Cover and bake at 350° for 1½ hours or until quick-registering meat thermometer registers 170°. Transfer roast to a serving platter. Drain vegetables, and place around roast. Slice and serve. Yield: 4 servings.

Ozark Pork Roast, a loin end cut, comes with root vegetables to serve as a one-dish meal.

CORN MEAL
GROUND AT

ROAST PORK AND SWEET POTATOES

1 (5- to 5½-pound) pork loin end roast
1 teaspoon salt
½ teaspoon pepper
4 gingersnap cookies, finely crushed
6 medium-size sweet potatoes
Butter or margarine

Rub roast with salt and pepper; dust with crushed gingersnaps. Place roast, fat side up, in a shallow roasting pan. Insert meat thermometer, being careful not to touch bone or fat.

Bake roast at 350° for 1 hour. Place sweet potatoes around roast; continue baking an additional 1½ hours or until meat thermometer registers 170°.

Transfer roast to a serving platter. Let stand 10 to 15 minutes before slicing. Split sweet potatoes, and serve with butter. Yield: 6 to 8 servings.

CROWN ROAST OF PORK WITH SAUSAGE STUFFING

3½ cups water, divided
1 tablespoon Worcestershire sauce
1 teaspoon commercial brown bouquet sauce
1 (6- to 7-pound) crown roast of pork
½ teaspoon salt
¼ teaspoon pepper
1 pound bulk pork sausage
1½ pounds new potatoes
⅓ cup all-purpose flour
Applesauce

Combine 1 cup water, Worcestershire sauce, and bouquet sauce; brush surface of roast with water mixture. Sprinkle with salt and pepper. Spoon sausage into center of roast. Place a small piece of aluminum foil on each bone end. Place roast, bone end up, in a shallow roasting pan. Pour remaining water mixture and 2 cups water over roast. Insert meat thermometer, being careful not to touch bone or fat.

Bake at 375° for 15 minutes; reduce heat to 325°, and bake 1 hour. Add potatoes to roasting pan, and continue baking 1 hour or until meat thermometer registers 170°. Remove roast and potatoes to a warm serving platter, reserving pan liquid. Let roast stand 10 to 15 minutes before slicing.

Degrease pan liquid; pour into a medium saucepan. Combine flour and remaining ½ cup water, stirring until smooth. Pour flour mixture into pan liquid; cook, stirring constantly, until thickened and bubbly. Serve gravy and applesauce with roast. Yield: 8 to 10 servings.

Children photographed as they watch the family pork supply on the hoof in Virginia, c.1920.

Valentine Museum, Richmond, Virginia

Collection of Business Americana

Colorful mustard label from the late nineteenth century.

PORK ROYAL

3 cups soft breadcrumbs, toasted
¼ cup plus 2 tablespoons butter or margarine, melted
1 tablespoon shortening, melted
¼ cup chopped onion
¾ teaspoon salt
¼ teaspoon pepper
½ teaspoon dried whole thyme
¼ teaspoon rubbed sage
1 (5½- to 6-pound) pork shoulder roast, boned and cut with pocket
¾ cup water
6 medium-size cooking apples, cored and partially peeled

Combine toasted breadcrumbs, butter, shortening, chopped onion, salt, pepper, thyme, and sage; mix well. Stuff pocket of roast with breadcrumb mixture; tie with string to secure opening.

Place roast and water in a lightly greased shallow roasting pan. Insert meat thermometer in thickest part of roast. Bake at 325° for 2 hours. Place apples around roast; bake 1 additional hour or until meat thermometer registers 170°. Baste apples occasionally with pan drippings.

Transfer roast and apples to a serving platter. Let roast stand 10 to 15 minutes before slicing. Yield: 6 servings.

MARINATED PORK TENDERLOIN

2 (¾-pound) pork tenderloins, trimmed
¼ cup soy sauce
¼ cup bourbon
2 tablespoons firmly packed brown sugar
Mustard Sauce

Place tenderloins in a large pan or dish. Combine soy sauce, bourbon, and sugar; stir well, and pour over tenderloins. Cover tightly and refrigerate several hours or overnight, turning meat several times. Drain, reserving marinade.

Place tenderloins on a greased rack in a shallow roasting pan. Insert meat thermometer in thickest part of meat. Bake at 325° for 1 hour and 15 minutes or until thermometer registers 170°. Baste every 15 minutes with marinade.

Transfer tenderloins to a warm serving platter. Cut into thin slices, and serve with Mustard Sauce. Yield: 6 servings.

Mustard Sauce:

⅓ cup commercial sour cream
⅓ cup mayonnaise
1 tablespoon dry mustard
2 green onions, chopped

Combine all ingredients in a small bowl; stir well. Cover and refrigerate until thoroughly chilled. Yield: ¾ cup.

PORK TENDERLOIN WITH SHERRIED APPLE RINGS

2 (1-pound) pork tenderloins, trimmed
1 teaspoon salt
¼ teaspoon pepper
Dash of sugar
¾ cup all-purpose flour
2 tablespoons bacon drippings
Sherried Apple Rings

Sprinkle tenderloins with salt, pepper, and sugar; dredge in flour. Insert meat thermometer in thickest part of meat.

Melt bacon drippings in a shallow roasting pan. Place tenderloins in pan; bake, uncovered, at 350° for 50 minutes or until thermometer registers 170°, basting occasionally.

Remove tenderloins to a serving platter, and arrange Sherried Apple Rings around meat. Spoon cooking liquid over apple rings. Slice meat and serve with apple rings. Yield: 6 servings.

Sherried Apple Rings:

4 small cooking apples
1 cup sugar
¾ cup sherry, divided
¼ cup water
1 teaspoon ground cinnamon
2 tablespoons lemon juice

Peel and core apples; cut into ½-inch-thick slices.

Combine sugar, ½ cup sherry, water, and cinnamon in a large skillet. Cook over low heat 5 minutes. Add apple slices; cover and simmer 3 minutes or until apples are tender. Remove from heat; add remaining ¼ cup sherry and lemon juice. Set aside to cool. Yield: 6 servings.

A mid-1800s kitchen with dinner in the preparation stage.

STOVE-TOP PORK BARBECUE

1 (5- to 6-pound) Boston Butt pork roast, trimmed
Bonaventure Barbecue Sauce

Randomly pierce surface of roast using a sharp knife. Place roast in a large Dutch oven. Pour Bonaventure Barbecue Sauce over roast; bring to a boil. Reduce heat; cover and simmer 2 hours or until meat is tender, basting roast with barbecue sauce and turning every 30 minutes during cooking time.

Transfer roast to a serving platter; slice and serve with barbecue sauce. Yield: 8 servings.

Bonaventure Barbecue Sauce:

2 cups water
1 cup catsup
¼ cup vinegar
¼ cup Worcestershire sauce
¼ cup firmly packed brown sugar
1 teaspoon salt
1 teaspoon celery seeds
1 teaspoon chili powder
3 drops hot sauce

Combine all ingredients in a saucepan; mix well. Bring to a boil. Reduce heat; simmer, uncovered, 15 minutes, stirring occasionally. Yield: 3½ cups.

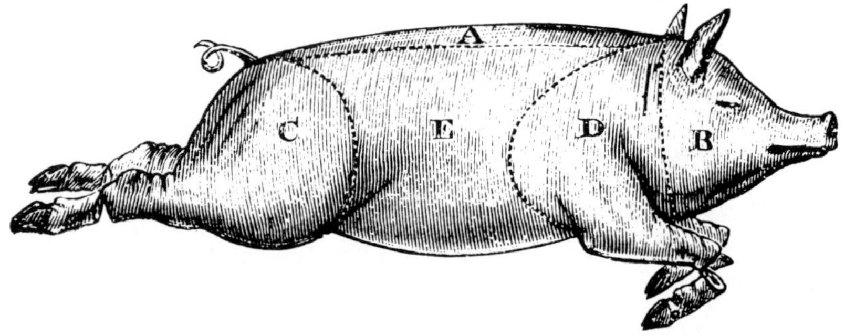

ARKANSAS LEG OF PORK

1 (15-pound) fresh ham
2 cloves garlic
1 dried red pepper, seeded
1 tablespoon vinegar
1 tablespoon coarsely ground black pepper
2 tablespoons prepared mustard
¼ cup plus 2 tablespoons fine dry breadcrumbs

Place ham, garlic, red pepper, vinegar, and water to cover in a large stock pot or kettle. Bring to a boil. Reduce heat; cover and simmer 5 hours or until ham is tender. Remove stock pot from heat; set aside. Allow ham to cool completely in cooking liquid in stock pot.

Drain ham well; remove fat. Discard cooking liquid and fat. Place ham in a large roasting pan. Rub surface of ham with pepper; brush with mustard. Sprinkle breadcrumbs over ham. Bake at 400° for 45 minutes or until browned. Cut into thin slices; serve hot or cold. Yield: 20 to 25 servings.

BROILED PORK TENDERLOIN

1 (1-pound) pork tenderloin, cut into ¼-inch-thick slices
2 tablespoons butter or margarine, melted
½ teaspoon salt

Place tenderloin slices on rack in broiler pan. Broil 3 to 4 inches from heating element 2 minutes on each side or until evenly browned on both sides. Brush with butter, and sprinkle with salt. Serve hot. Yield: 4 servings.

PORK TENDERLOIN WITH PRUNES

1½ cups dried pitted prunes
1 cup white wine
8 (1½-inch-thick) pork tenderloin slices (about 1½ pounds)
½ teaspoon salt
¼ teaspoon coarsely ground black pepper
3 tablespoons all-purpose flour
3 tablespoons butter or margarine
½ cup chicken broth
½ cup whipping cream
2 teaspoons red currant jelly
Maraschino cherries (optional)

Combine prunes and wine in a small saucepan; cover and let stand at room temperature overnight. Bring prune mixture to a boil. Reduce heat, and simmer 10 minutes. Drain prunes, reserving liquid. Set prunes and liquid aside.

Sprinkle pork with salt, pepper, and flour. Brown on all sides in butter in a large skillet over medium heat. Drain pork on paper towels; reserve 1 tablespoon pan drippings in skillet. Add reserved prune liquid, chicken broth, and pork to skillet. Bring to a boil. Reduce heat; cover and simmer 40 minutes or until pork is tender.

Remove pork to a warmed serving platter; reserve liquid in skillet. Stir in whipping cream; cook over low heat 3 minutes or until slightly thickened, stirring constantly. Add jelly; stir until dissolved. Stir in prunes; cook over low heat until hot. Place prunes around pork on platter; pour sauce over top. Garnish with maraschino cherries, if desired. Yield: 4 servings.

BROILED PORK STEAKS

4 (½-inch-thick) pork shoulder steaks (about 2½ pounds)
¾ teaspoon salt
¼ teaspoon pepper
¼ teaspoon dried whole sage
Applesauce

Place steaks on rack in broiler pan. Place pan 6 to 7 inches from heating element. Broil 10 minutes on first side; turn steaks. Sprinkle with salt, pepper, and sage; broil second side 10 minutes. Place steaks on a warm platter, and serve with applesauce. Yield: 4 servings.

PORK STEAKS WITH RAISIN DRESSING

6 (½-inch-thick) pork steaks (about 2½ pounds)
1½ teaspoons salt, divided
2 tablespoons shortening
3 cups soft bread cubes, toasted
1½ cups chopped, unpeeled apple
½ cup raisins
½ cup chopped celery
½ cup chopped onion
¼ teaspoon pepper
1 teaspoon poultry seasoning
1 beef-flavored bouillon cube
½ cup hot water
2 medium-size cooking apples, cored and sliced
Sugar

Sprinkle steaks with ½ teaspoon salt. Brown steaks on both sides in hot shortening in a large skillet; drain.

Combine bread cubes, chopped apple, raisins, celery, onion, 1 teaspoon salt, pepper, and poultry seasoning in a medium mixing bowl; stir until well combined. Dissolve bouillon cube in hot water, and add to breadcrumb mixture, mixing well.

Place browned steaks in a 3½-quart shallow baking dish. Cover each steak with a layer of dressing and top with an apple slice. Sprinkle with sugar. Cover dish tightly with aluminum foil, and bake at 350° for 1 hour. Serve immediately. Yield: 6 servings.

BAKED PORK STEAKS

6 (½-inch-thick) Boston Butt pork steaks (about 1½ pounds)
2 tablespoons shortening, melted
1½ teaspoons salt
¼ teaspoon pepper
1 cup regular rice, uncooked
3½ cups chicken broth
½ cup chopped green onion
¼ teaspoon poultry seasoning

Brown pork steaks on both sides in hot shortening in a large skillet; drain steaks, reserving pan drippings in skillet. Sprinkle steaks on both sides with salt and pepper. Set aside.

Add rice to pan drippings; cook over medium heat 10 minutes or until lightly browned, stirring constantly. Add chicken broth, onion, and poultry seasoning to rice; stir well. Pour rice mixture into a well-greased 3-quart casserole; place pork steaks on top of rice mixture. Cover and bake at 350° for 1 hour and 20 minutes or until liquid is absorbed. Serve hot. Yield: 6 servings.

PORK STEAK FRICASSEE

6 (½-inch-thick) pork steaks (about 3 pounds)
¼ cup vegetable oil
¼ cup all-purpose flour
1 medium onion, chopped
1 medium-size green pepper, chopped
1½ cups water
1 teaspoon salt
½ teaspoon pepper
2 to 3 green onions, chopped
Hot cooked rice

Trim excess fat from steaks, and slice into 4- x 1-inch strips. Sauté strips in hot oil in a large skillet until browned. Remove steak from skillet; drain. Reserve drippings.

Add flour to drippings; stir until well blended. Cook, stirring constantly, over medium heat until mixture is browned. Add onion and green pepper; cook over low heat 3 minutes, stirring constantly. Add water, salt, and pepper; stir until smooth. Add browned steak; cover and cook over medium heat 30 minutes. Stir in green onion; cover and cook an additional 10 minutes. Remove from heat, and serve over rice. Yield: 6 servings.

Mary Frances Henderson, in *Practical Cooking, and Dinner Giving*, 1876, gave a recipe for "roast little pig," saying, "Anyone who fancies can cook a little pig, not I." Once the pig grew up, however, the lady felt free to poke up the fire and start cooking; she includes several recipes for pork. A dish of Broiled Pork Cutlets was made like this: "Cut six cutlets off each neck, taking them a little obliquely; trim them, season, and roll them in melted butter and bread-crumbs. Broil them. Pour into a stew pan 4 or 5 tablespoons of vinegar, and double its volume of stock or gravy; let it boil, and thicken it with a little flour. Pass it through a sieve, and add to it pepper and some spoonfuls of chopped pickles. Dish the cutlets in a circle, and pour over them the sauce. . . ." At times she fried the cutlets.

Pork Cutlets

Cut them from the leg and remove the skin; trim and beat them and sprinkle them with pepper and salt. Prepare some beaten egg in a pan and on a

A recipe from the Blackford family papers, Virginia, 1852.

Blackford Family Papers, University of North Carolina at Chapel Hill

Broiled Pork Chops with Robert Sauce, served with noodles and garnished with a drift of fresh dill.

BROILED PORK CHOPS WITH ROBERT SAUCE

4 (¾-inch-thick) pork loin chops (about 1¼ pounds)
½ teaspoon salt
¼ teaspoon pepper
Hot cooked noodles
Robert Sauce

Sprinkle chops with salt and pepper. Place on rack in broiler pan 3 to 4 inches from heat. Broil 5 to 6 minutes on first side; turn and broil 3 minutes or until browned. Transfer chops to a warm serving platter of hot cooked noodles. Reserve 2 tablespoons pan drippings for Robert Sauce. Spoon Robert Sauce over chops and noodles. Yield: 4 servings.

Robert Sauce:

3 tablespoons chopped yellow onion
1 tablespoon butter or margarine
2 tablespoons tarragon vinegar
2 tablespoons pan drippings
2 tablespoons all-purpose flour
1 cup milk
2 tablespoons Dijon mustard
1 teaspoon salt
¼ teaspoon pepper

Sauté onion in butter in a medium saucepan until tender; add vinegar, and bring to a boil. Combine drippings, flour, and milk in a small bowl; gradually add to vinegar mixture. Stir in mustard, salt, and pepper; boil 10 minutes, stirring frequently. Yield: about 1 cup.

FRIED PORK CHOPS

6 (⅜-inch-thick) pork loin chops (about 1 pound)
¼ cup all-purpose flour
½ teaspoon salt
¼ teaspoon pepper
¾ cup vegetable oil

Trim exterior fat from chops, and place chops in a paper or plastic bag with flour, salt, and pepper; shake to mix.

Heat oil in 10-inch skillet over high heat. Cook chops 2 to 3 minutes or until lightly browned on both sides. Drain on paper towels, and serve immediately. Yield: 6 servings.

BRAISED PORK CHOPS

4 (¾-inch-thick) pork loin chops (about 1½ pounds)
½ teaspoon salt
¼ teaspoon pepper
¼ cup all-purpose flour
¼ cup vegetable oil
½ cup water
Fresh parsley sprigs (optional)

Sprinkle chops with salt and pepper; dredge in flour. Sauté chops in oil in a heavy skillet over medium heat 4 minutes on each side or until golden brown. Add water; cover and cook over low heat 45 minutes or until chops are tender. Remove chops to a warm serving platter, and garnish with parsley sprigs, if desired. Yield: 4 servings.

PORK CHOPS AND GRAVY

½ cup plus 1 tablespoon all-purpose flour, divided
½ teaspoon salt
¼ teaspoon pepper
6 (½-inch-thick) pork chops (about 1¾ pounds)
2 tablespoons lard or shortening
2 medium onions, chopped
1 clove garlic, minced
1 tablespoon minced celery
2½ cups water
1 tablespoon minced parsley
Pinch of dried whole thyme
1 large bay leaf

Combine ½ cup flour, salt, and pepper; dredge chops in flour mixture. Heat lard in a large skillet; add chops, and brown on both sides over medium heat. Remove chops from skillet; drain on paper towels. Reserve pan drippings in skillet.

Sauté onion and garlic in pan drippings until tender. Add celery, and cook over medium heat 5 minutes, stirring frequently. Add remaining flour, stirring until well blended. Cook an additional 3 minutes.

Return chops to skillet, and add water. Stir in parsley, thyme, and bay leaf. Bring to a boil. Reduce heat; cover and simmer 30 minutes. Uncover and simmer an additional 30 minutes or until chops are tender.

Remove and discard bay leaf. Transfer chops to serving plates, and spoon pan gravy over each. Yield: 6 servings.

PORK CHOPS IN VERMOUTH

3 tablespoons vegetable oil
4 (1½-inch-thick) pork loin chops (about 2½-pounds)
½ teaspoon salt
½ teaspoon rubbed sage
½ teaspoon paprika
½ cup beef broth
1 clove garlic
½ cup dry vermouth
½ cup commercial sour cream

Heat oil in a 10-inch cast-iron skillet; brown chops on both sides over high heat. Sprinkle chops with salt, sage, and paprika; pour off pan drippings. Drain chops on paper towels.

Return chops to skillet; add beef broth and garlic. Cover and simmer over low heat until tender. Remove chops, and set aside. Add vermouth and sour cream to broth in skillet, stirring well.

Return chops to sauce, and cook over low heat 15 minutes, turning chops and basting frequently with sauce. Serve immediately with sauce. Yield: 4 servings.

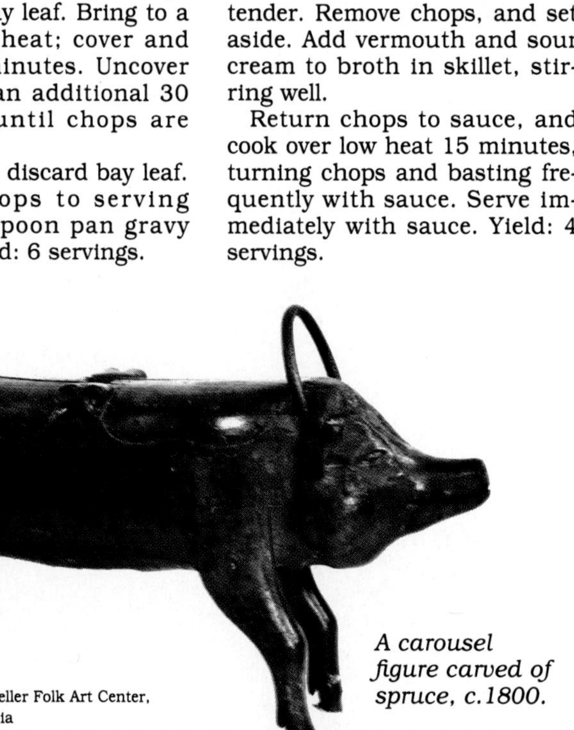

Abby Aldrich Rockefeller Folk Art Center, Williamsburg, Virginia

A carousel figure carved of spruce, c.1800.

BAKED STUFFED PORK CHOPS

1 (6½-ounce) package commercial cornbread mix
6 baked biscuits
2 eggs, slightly beaten
1 teaspoon rubbed sage
½ teaspoon salt
½ teaspoon pepper
1 cup chopped onion
1 cup chopped celery
2 cups chicken broth
1 tablespoon butter or margarine, melted
3 tablespoons vegetable oil
Salt and pepper to taste
6 (1½-inch-thick) pork loin chops, cut with pockets
Honey Glaze

Prepare cornbread according to package directions; remove cornbread from skillet, and cool on wire rack.

Crumble cornbread and biscuits in a large mixing bowl; stir in eggs, sage, salt, and pepper. Set aside.

Combine onion, celery, chicken broth, and butter in a medium saucepan; cook over medium heat until vegetables are tender. Add to cornbread mixture; mix well, and set aside.

Heat oil in a large skillet over high heat. Sprinkle salt and pepper to taste on pork chops, and heavily brown in oil on both sides. Drain on paper towels.

Stuff pockets of pork chops with stuffing. Place remaining stuffing in a lightly greased 10- x 6- x 2-inch baking dish. Bake, uncovered, at 350° for 35 minutes or until golden brown.

Place pork chops in a lightly greased 13- x 9- x 2-inch baking dish. Bake, uncovered, at 350° for 40 minutes or until tender. Baste frequently with Honey Glaze. Serve with baked stuffing. Yield: 6 servings.

Honey Glaze:

1 cup honey
1 tablespoon firmly packed brown sugar
1 tablespoon soy sauce

Combine all ingredients in small mixing bowl; stir well. Yield: about 1 cup.

OVEN-BARBECUED PORK CHOPS

6 (½-inch-thick) pork loin chops
1 teaspoon salt
⅛ teaspoon pepper
½ cup water
¼ cup vinegar
¼ cup chili sauce
3 tablespoons firmly packed brown sugar
2 tablespoons dry mustard

Sprinkle pork chops with salt and pepper; place in a greased 13- x 9- x 2-inch baking dish, and set aside.

Combine water, vinegar, chili sauce, sugar, and mustard; mix well. Pour sauce over pork chops. Cover and bake at 400° for 1 hour. Uncover and continue baking 30 minutes.

Remove chops to a serving platter. Pour remaining sauce over chops. Yield: 6 servings.

CRANBERRY-GLAZED PORK CHOPS

1 cup water
1 cup sugar
2 cups fresh cranberries
6 (1-inch-thick) pork chops (about 2½ pounds)
½ cup all-purpose flour
2 tablespoons butter or margarine
6 medium-size sweet potatoes (optional)

Combine water and sugar in a medium saucepan; bring to a boil. Reduce heat; simmer 10 minutes. Add cranberries; bring to a boil. Remove from heat, and set aside.

Dredge pork chops in flour. Brown in butter in a large skillet. Drain chops; place in a 13- x 9- x 2-inch baking dish. Pour glaze over chops.

Cover; bake at 350° for 30 minutes. Uncover, and bake 30 minutes or until chops are tender. Cook potatoes in oven with chops at 350° for 1 hour, if desired. Transfer chops to a serving platter. Spoon glaze over chops. Serve with potatoes, if desired. Yield: 6 servings.

This recipe for "Pork Fritters," dated 1893, charms with its deceptive simplicity: "Have at hand a thick batter of Indian meal and flour; cut a few slices of pork and fry until the fat is fried out; cut a few more slices of the pork, dip them in the batter, and drop them in the bubbling fat, seasoning with salt and pepper. Cook light brown and eat while hot."

Cranberry-Glazed Pork Chops complemented by baked sweet potatoes.

This photograph made near Palm Beach, Florida, c.1910, shows men at work in the pineapple harvest.

PORK CHOPS WITH FRIED APPLES

1 egg
¼ cup milk
1 teaspoon salt
⅛ teaspoon pepper
Dash of rubbed sage
6 (½-inch-thick) pork chops (about 1½ pounds)
1 cup all-purpose flour
Vegetable oil
1 cup milk
3 medium-size cooking apples, unpeeled, cored, and sliced
½ cup sugar
Hot biscuits (optional)

Combine first 5 ingredients in a shallow dish; beat well. Dip chops in egg mixture; dredge in flour. Reserve 2 tablespoons flour for gravy.

Heat ½ inch oil in a large skillet to 350°. Add pork chops; fry until golden brown and tender, turning as needed. Drain chops; transfer to a warm serving platter. Reserve pan drippings in skillet.

Transfer 2 tablespoons pan drippings to a small skillet; add reserved flour, stirring until smooth. Cook 1 minute, stirring constantly. Gradually add milk; cook over medium heat, stirring constantly, until thickened and bubbly. Pour gravy into serving bowl.

Fry apple slices in remaining reserved hot pan drippings until tender, turning once. Drain well on paper towels. Sprinkle apple slices with sugar. To serve, arrange fried apple slices around pork chops, and serve with gravy and hot biscuits, if desired. Yield: 6 servings.

Pork Chops with Fried Apples (front) and Autumn Baked Pork Chops topped with acorn squash rings.

PINEAPPLE PORK CHOPS

1 (8-ounce) can pineapple chunks, undrained
5 slices white bread, cubed
¼ cup chopped onion
¼ cup chopped celery
3 tablespoons butter or margarine, melted
1 teaspoon salt, divided
¼ teaspoon rubbed sage
⅛ teaspoon ground cinnamon
6 (½-inch-thick) pork chops (about 1½ pounds)

Drain pineapple, reserving 2 tablespoons juice. Combine pineapple chunks, bread cubes, onion, celery, butter, ½ teaspoon salt, sage, and cinnamon in a large bowl, mixing well. Set stuffing mixture aside.

Place pork chops in a 13- x 9- x 2-inch baking dish; sprinkle with reserved pineapple juice and remaining salt. Top pork chops evenly with stuffing mixture. Cover and bake at 350° for 30 minutes. Uncover, and bake an additional 15 minutes or until chops are tender. Yield: 6 servings.

AUTUMN BAKED PORK CHOPS

4 (1-inch-thick) pork loin chops (about 2 pounds)
2 tablespoons shortening
4 (1-inch-thick) acorn squash rings, peeled
12 dried apricots
8 dried prunes
½ teaspoon salt
3 tablespoons grated orange rind
½ cup orange juice

Brown pork chops in hot shortening in a large skillet. Remove chops from skillet; drain.

Place pork chops in a well-greased 2½-quart shallow baking dish. Place an acorn squash ring on top of each chop. Fill center of each ring with three apricots and two prunes. Sprinkle pork chops with salt.

Combine orange rind and juice; pour over chops. Cover and bake at 350° for 1 hour and 15 minutes or until pork chops are tender; baste occasionally with pan drippings. Transfer chops to a warmed serving platter. Yield: 4 servings.

ONE-DISH PORK CHOPS

2 tablespoons shortening
6 (¾-inch-thick) pork chops (about 2 pounds)
2 teaspoons salt, divided
¾ teaspoon pepper, divided
¼ cup plus 2 tablespoons regular rice, uncooked and divided
1 large tomato, sliced
1 large onion, sliced
1 large green pepper, seeded and sliced into rings
2 cups tomato juice
¼ cup water

Melt shortening in a large skillet over medium heat.

Sprinkle pork chops with 1 teaspoon salt and ¼ teaspoon pepper, and brown on both sides in oil. Drain chops on paper towels, and pour off remaining grease in skillet.

Return pork chops to skillet. Place 1 tablespoon rice and 1 slice tomato, onion, and green pepper on each. Cover layers with tomato juice and water. Sprinkle with 1 teaspoon salt and ½ teaspoon pepper. Cover and bring to a boil. Reduce heat, and simmer 45 minutes. Transfer chops to a serving platter, and serve immediately. Yield: 6 servings.

Pork chops received short shrift in the old cookbooks as a rule. One recipe from 1893 says only, "Fry or stew pork chops, after taking off the rind or skin, the same as for veal." One suspects the pork chop was lost in the shuffle at butchering time, perhaps when the tenderloin and rib roasts were cut. One matter has remained the same, however: With pork of every cut, the accompaniments of choice have been applesauce and sauerkraut.

Ad for N.K. Fairbank & Company's lard.

BAKED CHOPS WITH VEGETABLES

2 tablespoons shortening
6 (¾-inch-thick) pork loin chops (about 2 pounds)
1 medium-size green pepper, chopped
1 small onion, chopped
1 cup chopped celery
¼ cup plus 2 tablespoons butter or margarine, divided
1 (8¾-ounce) can whole kernel corn, drained
1 cup soft breadcrumbs
1 egg, beaten
1 teaspoon salt
¼ teaspoon pepper
3 tablespoons all-purpose flour
1 cup milk

Melt shortening in a large skillet over medium heat; add pork chops, and brown on both sides. Remove chops from skillet, and drain on paper towels; drain off pan drippings.

Sauté green pepper, onion, and celery in ¼ cup butter in a medium saucepan. Remove from heat; add corn, breadcrumbs, egg, salt, and pepper, stirring until well blended. Set vegetable mixture aside.

Melt remaining butter in a heavy saucepan over low heat; add flour, stirring until smooth. Cook 1 minute, stirring constantly. Gradually add milk; cook over medium heat, stirring constantly, until thickened and bubbly.

Arrange pork chops in a lightly greased 13- x 9- x 2-inch baking dish. Spoon vegetable mixture over pork chops. Pour white sauce evenly over vegetable mixture. Bake, uncovered, at 300° for 45 minutes or until pork chops are tender. Serve immediately. Yield: 6 servings.

CREOLE PORK CHOPS

- 6 (1-inch-thick) pork loin chops (about 2½ pounds)
- ½ cup all-purpose flour
- 2 tablespoons vegetable oil
- 1 medium onion, chopped
- ½ cup chopped green pepper
- 1 (14½-ounce) can whole tomatoes, undrained and chopped
- 1½ teaspoons Worcestershire sauce
- 1 teaspoon salt
- ¼ teaspoon pepper
- Hot cooked rice

Dredge pork chops in flour; brown on both sides in oil in a large skillet over medium heat. Drain on paper towels. Remove drippings from skillet, reserving 1 tablespoon in skillet.

Sauté onion and green pepper in hot drippings until tender. Add tomatoes, Worcestershire sauce, salt, and pepper. Return pork chops to skillet. Cover and simmer 1 hour or until pork chops are tender. Serve over rice. Yield: 6 servings.

PORK AND SAUERKRAUT DINNER

- 4 slices bacon
- ¼ cup chopped onion
- 1 (16-ounce) can shredded sauerkraut, drained
- 1 medium carrot, scraped and sliced
- 1½ teaspoons sugar
- 3 whole peppercorns
- 1 whole clove
- 1 small bay leaf
- Cheeesecloth
- ¼ cup plus 2 tablespoons chicken broth
- ¼ cup Chablis or other dry white wine
- 2 medium potatoes, peeled and quartered
- 2 (½-inch-thick) smoked pork chops (about ¾ pound)
- 2 (¼-pound) knockwurst sausages, diagonally scored

Cook bacon in a 9-inch cast-iron skillet until crisp; drain on paper towels. Crumble and set aside, reserving 1½ tablespoons drippings in skillet.

Sauté onion in drippings until tender. Add sauerkraut, carrot, sugar, and crumbled bacon, stirring gently until well blended.

Combine peppercorns, clove, and bay leaf on a small amount of cheesecloth, and tie securely. Place cheesecloth bag in skillet, and cover completely with sauerkraut mixture.

Pour chicken broth and wine over sauerkraut mixture; bring to a boil. Reduce heat; cover and simmer 10 minutes. Place potatoes, pork chops, and sausages evenly over sauerkraut. Cover and simmer 1 hour. Discard cheesecloth bag.

To serve, place sauerkraut mixture on a warm serving platter. Arrange pork chops, sausages, and potatoes on top of sauerkraut. Serve immediately. Yield: 4 servings.

Label from a large can of Deer brand sauerkraut includes a bucolic scene of cabbages growing in the Rio Grande Valley of Texas.

FINGER-LICKIN' RIBS

SPARERIBS WITH GRAVY

2 to 2½ pounds pork spareribs, cut into 4 serving-size pieces
2 teaspoons salt
¼ teaspoon pepper
1 tablespoon Worcestershire sauce
1 teaspoon commercial brown bouquet sauce
1 large onion, quartered
½ cup coarsely chopped celery leaves
1 clove garlic, quartered
Cheesecloth
3 tablespoons all-purpose flour
⅓ cup water
Hot cooked grits (optional)

Combine spareribs and water to cover in a large Dutch oven. Add salt, pepper, Worcestershire sauce, and bouquet sauce; stir well. Combine onion, celery leaves, and garlic; tie securely in cheesecloth. Place cheesecloth bag in sparerib mixture. Bring to a boil; cover and simmer 2 hours or until ribs are tender.

Remove spareribs to a warm serving platter and cover. Discard cheesecloth bag, and reserve 2 cups cooking liquid in Dutch oven.

Combine flour and ⅓ cup water; stir until smooth. Pour flour mixture into reserved cooking liquid; cook, stirring constantly, until thickened and bubbly. Pour gravy over warm spareribs, and serve immediately with hot cooked grits, if desired. Yield: about 2 to 4 servings.

BROILED RIBS

4 pounds pork spareribs, cut into 4 serving-size pieces
1 teaspoon salt
½ teaspoon pepper
½ cup butter or margarine, melted
¼ cup molasses

Sprinkle both sides of spareribs with salt and pepper. Place ribs in a well-greased shallow roasting pan. Pour butter and molasses over ribs. Broil ribs 7 to 8 inches from heating element, 20 minutes on each side; baste frequently with pan drippings. Yield: 4 servings.

Houston Metropolitan Research Center

SWEET-AND-SOUR SPARERIBS

2 pounds pork spareribs
3 tablespoons firmly packed brown sugar
Cheesecloth
1½ cups vinegar

Place ribs on rack in a broiler pan 6 to 7 inches from heating element. Broil 2 minutes.

Place sugar in cheesecloth, and tie securely. Dip into vinegar. Rub cheesecloth bag over ribs several times. Continue broiling ribs 8 minutes, basting frequently. Turn ribs, and broil an additional 8 minutes, basting with sugar bag. Cut ribs into serving-size pieces. Yield: 2 servings.

ROASTED SPARERIBS

¼ cup chopped onion
2 tablespoons chopped celery
2 tablespoons butter or margarine
1 cup cooked, mashed potatoes
¾ cup soft breadcrumbs
1 egg, beaten
1 tablespoon chopped fresh parsley
¼ teaspoon dried whole marjoram
¼ teaspoon salt
Dash of pepper
2 pounds pork spareribs (two rib sections)
½ teaspoon salt
¼ teaspoon pepper
½ cup water

Sauté onion and celery in butter in a skillet until tender. Stir in potatoes, breadcrumbs, egg, parsley, marjoram, ¼ teaspoon salt, and dash of pepper.

Place stuffing on one half of sparerib slab. Fold remaining half over stuffing; secure with wooden picks. Sprinkle spareribs with remaining salt and pepper. Bake at 450°, uncovered, for 30 minutes. Reduce heat to 350°; pour water around spareribs. Cover; bake for 1 hour or until tender. Remove wooden picks. Cut into serving-size pieces. Yield: 2 servings.

DEEP SOUTH OVEN-BARBECUED RIBS

6 pounds pork loin country-style ribs, cut into serving-size pieces
1 large onion, sliced
1 lemon, sliced
Deep South Barbecue Sauce

Place ribs in a lightly greased shallow roasting pan. Cover and bake at 450° for 45 minutes. Drain off drippings. Place onion and lemon slices over ribs; pour Deep South Barbecue Sauce over top. Reduce heat to 350°, and continue baking, uncovered, 40 minutes or until sauce has thickened. Baste ribs with sauce frequently. Yield: 8 to 10 servings.

Deep South Barbecue Sauce:

3 cloves garlic, minced
2 tablespoons butter or margarine
1½ cups water
1 cup catsup
¾ cup chili sauce
¼ cup firmly packed brown sugar
2 tablespoons Worcestershire sauce
2 tablespoons soy sauce
2 tablespoons prepared mustard
1 tablespoon celery seeds
2 teaspoons chili powder
½ teaspoon salt
¼ teaspoon liquid smoke
Hot sauce to taste

Sauté garlic in butter in a medium saucepan. Combine remaining ingredients; mix well. Bring to a boil. Reduce heat; simmer, uncovered, 15 minutes, stirring occasionally. Yield: 4 cups.

STUFFED BAKED SPARERIBS

1 cup finely chopped apples
1 cup soft breadcrumbs
½ cup finely chopped onion
1 tablespoon firmly packed brown sugar
¾ teaspoon salt, divided
¼ teaspoon pepper, divided
4 pounds pork spareribs (two rib sections)
¼ teaspoon rubbed sage
Fresh parsley sprigs
Spiced crabapples

Combine first 6 ingredients; mix well.

Place one rib section on a lightly greased rack in a shallow roasting pan. Spoon stuffing over ribs. Place remaining rib section over stuffing; tie rib sections together. Sprinkle remaining salt, pepper, and sage over ribs. Bake, uncovered, at 475° for 20 minutes. Reduce heat to 325°; cover and bake 1 hour. Transfer ribs to a serving platter. Garnish with parsley and crabapples. Cut rib sections into individual ribs with stuffing. Yield: 4 servings.

SHERRIED SPARERIBS

3 pounds pork spareribs
½ cup sherry
¼ cup plus 2 tablespoons catsup
¼ cup plus 2 tablespoons water
1 tablespoon firmly packed brown sugar
1 tablespoon white wine vinegar
1 tablespoon Worcestershire sauce
¾ teaspoon salt
¼ teaspoon pepper
⅛ teaspoon chili powder
⅛ teaspoon red pepper

Cut ribs into serving-size pieces; place on a lightly greased rack in a shallow roasting pan. Bake, uncovered, at 425° for 30 minutes.

Combine remaining ingredients in a medium saucepan; bring to a boil, stirring well.

Place roasting pan 7 to 8 inches from heating element. Broil ribs 15 minutes, turning every 5 minutes; baste liberally with sauce. Serve remaining sauce with spareribs. Yield: about 4 servings.

Stuffed Baked Spareribs enclose a flavorful mixture of apples, onion, and breadcrumbs to make a hearty dinner dish.

The Historic New Orleans Collection, 533 Royal Street

Butchers at their stalls in New Orleans' French Market, Vieux Carré, 1892.

PORK RIB JAMBALAYA

2 pounds pork spareribs, trimmed
¼ cup vegetable oil
1 medium onion, chopped
1 small green pepper, seeded and chopped
½ cup chopped green onion
½ cup chopped fresh parsley
2 cups regular rice, uncooked
1 teaspoon salt
¼ teaspoon pepper

Brown ribs in oil in a large Dutch oven over high heat. Drain well on paper towels. Reserve drippings in Dutch oven.

Sauté chopped onion, green pepper, and green onion in remaining drippings 2 minutes. Return browned ribs to Dutch oven; add remaining ingredients and water to cover. Cover and cook over low heat 20 minutes or until water is absorbed. Serve immediately. Yield: 2 to 4 servings.

SPARERIBS AND SAUERKRAUT

4 to 4½ pounds pork spareribs
3 tablespoons shortening, melted
1½ teaspoons salt
½ teaspoon pepper
1 medium onion, sliced
2 stalks celery, coarsely chopped
1 (28-ounce) can shredded sauerkraut, undrained
1 teaspoon caraway seeds
1 teaspoon sugar

Have butcher cut rib section lengthwise into serving pieces. Brown spareribs slightly on both sides in shortening in a large skillet over medium heat. Drain well.

Sprinkle ribs on both sides with salt and pepper. Place ribs in a large Dutch oven; add water to cover, onion, and celery. Cover and cook over low heat 1½ hours or until ribs are tender. Drain well.

Place sauerkraut, caraway seeds, and sugar in bottom of Dutch oven; stir well. Place ribs over sauerkraut; cover and cook over low heat 30 minutes. To serve, arrange sauerkraut on a serving platter, and place ribs over top. Yield: 4 to 6 servings.

OLD DOMINION PORK AND SAUERKRAUT

1½ pounds pork loin country-style ribs, cut into serving-size pieces
3 (16-ounce) cans chopped sauerkraut, undrained
Hot biscuits

Place ribs in a lightly greased 2½-quart shallow baking dish. Add sauerkraut to baking dish, completely covering and surrounding ribs. Cover; bake at 350° for 1 hour and 45 minutes. Transfer sauerkraut and ribs to a warm serving platter. Serve with hot biscuits. Yield: about 4 servings.

PORK AND TURNIPS OVER RICE

1 pound lean boneless pork, cut into 1-inch cubes
1¼ teaspoons salt, divided
½ teaspoon pepper
2 cups peeled, diced turnips
1 tablespoon sugar
4 cups water, divided
1½ tablespoons vegetable oil
2 tablespoons all-purpose flour
1 medium onion, chopped
1 clove garlic, minced
¼ teaspoon dried whole rosemary
⅛ teaspoon red pepper
Hot cooked rice

Sprinkle pork with 1 teaspoon salt and pepper. Set aside.

Combine turnips, sugar, and 2 cups water in a heavy saucepan. Bring to a boil; reduce heat, and simmer 10 minutes. Drain and set aside.

Combine oil and flour in a large Dutch oven; cook over medium heat, stirring frequently, 5 minutes or until golden brown. Stir in onion and garlic; cook until onion is tender. Add pork and remaining water; stir well. Bring to a boil. Reduce heat; cover and simmer 1 hour or until pork is tender. Stir in rosemary, remaining salt, and red pepper. Cover; simmer 10 minutes. Serve pork and turnips over rice. Yield: 6 servings.

OVEN-BARBECUED PORK CUBES

3 pounds boneless lean pork, cut into 2-inch cubes
2 tablespoons shortening, melted
1 teaspoon salt
¼ teaspoon pepper
1 (8-ounce) can tomato sauce
1 medium onion, sliced
½ cup chopped celery
½ cup water
½ cup catsup
2 tablespoons firmly packed brown sugar
2 tablespoons prepared mustard
1 tablespoon Worcestershire sauce
Hot cooked rice

Brown pork in shortening in a heavy skillet over medium heat; drain well.

Place pork in a large Dutch oven; sprinkle with salt and pepper. Add tomato sauce, onion, celery, water, catsup, brown sugar, mustard, and Worcestershire sauce; stir well. Cover and cook over low heat 2 hours and 10 minutes. Uncover and simmer an additional 20 minutes, stirring occasionally. Serve over rice. Yield: 4 to 6 servings.

PAPRIKA PORK

1 pound lean boneless pork, cut into ¾-inch cubes
2 teaspoons lard or shortening
1 teaspoon salt
1 teaspoon paprika
1 cup chopped celery
1 cup chopped onion
2 tablespoons molasses
Hot cooked rice

Sauté pork cubes in lard in a large skillet; add salt and paprika, mixing well. Stir in celery, onion, and molasses. Add water to cover. Cook mixture, covered, over medium heat 30 minutes. Reduce heat; uncover and cook an additional 15 minutes, stirring mixture frequently. Serve over hot cooked rice. Yield: 4 servings.

A merchant's sign made especially for a butcher's shop, c.1835.

National Gallery of Art

SWEET-AND-SOUR PORK

¼ cup all-purpose flour
1 teaspoon salt
Dash of pepper
3 tablespoons milk
1 egg
1 pound lean boneless pork, cut into 1-inch cubes
Vegetable oil
1 (8-ounce) can pineapple chunks, undrained
1 large green pepper, seeded and cut into 1½-inch cubes
1 cup chicken broth, divided
½ cup firmly packed brown sugar
3 tablespoons vinegar
2 teaspoons soy sauce
2 tablespoons cornstarch
1 small tomato, quartered
Hot cooked rice

Combine flour, salt, pepper, milk, and egg; beat until smooth. Dip pork cubes in batter, coating well; deep fry in hot oil (375°) for 5 minutes or until golden brown. Drain and set aside.

Drain pineapple, reserving 2 tablespoons juice. Combine pineapple chunks, juice, green pepper, ¾ cup chicken broth, brown sugar, vinegar, and soy sauce in a large skillet. Bring to a boil.

Combine cornstarch and remaining chicken broth, stirring until smooth; stir into pineapple mixture. Cook over medium heat until thickened and bubbly. Stir in pork and tomato. Serve immediately over rice. Yield: 4 servings.

Sweet-and-Sour Pork with hot rice lends an Oriental flair to the South's favorite meat.

PORK CHOP SUEY

1 pound lean boneless pork, diced
2 tablespoons vegetable oil
1 cup diced onion
1 cup diced celery
1¼ cups water, divided
2 tablespoons cornstarch
2 tablespoons bead molasses
¼ cup plus 2 tablespoons soy sauce
1 (14-ounce) can bean sprouts, drained
1 (8-ounce) can water chestnuts, drained
Hot cooked rice
1 (3-ounce) can Chinese noodles

Sauté pork in oil in a large skillet until color changes on all sides (do not brown). Add onion and celery; sauté until tender. Add 1 cup water, and bring to a boil. Reduce heat; cover and simmer 5 minutes.

Combine remaining ¼ cup water, cornstarch, and molasses; stir until smooth. Add cornstarch mixture and soy sauce to pork. Cook, stirring constantly, until thickened and bubbly. Add bean sprouts and water chestnuts; cover and simmer an additional 5 minutes. Serve over rice, and garnish with noodles. Yield: 4 to 6 servings.

One of the happiest aspects of cookery is that we feel free to play fast and loose with ingredients. That is how Americans invented chop suey. Yes, we did. According to Helen Lang, Louisville's authority on Chinese cuisine, the word suey means simply mixture or mélange, and refers to the topping. We can put anything we wish into it, and serve it on anything from rice to noodles. Chow mein really is a Chinese dish; we do take liberties.

PORK AND CORN CASSEROLE

1 medium onion, chopped
1 clove garlic, minced
2 tablespoons vegetable oil
¾ pound lean boneless pork, cut into ½-inch cubes
1 tablespoon chopped red jalapeño pepper
½ teaspoon salt
¼ teaspoon pepper
6 ears tender, young corn, cleaned and kernels cut from cob

Sauté onion and garlic in oil in a heavy skillet until tender. Add pork, chopped pepper, salt, and pepper; cook over medium heat, stirring frequently, until pork is browned.

Layer half of corn in a lightly greased 1-quart casserole. Spoon pork mixture over corn, and top with remaining corn. Bake, uncovered, at 350° for 30 minutes. Yield: 4 servings.

POSOLE ORTIZ

1 pound boneless pork shoulder, cubed
2 cups white hominy
1 quart water
⅓ cup chopped onion
1 tablespoon crushed red pepper
1 teaspoon whole peppercorns
⅛ teaspoon dried whole oregano
Salt to taste

Combine all ingredients in a large Dutch oven, and bring mixture to a boil. Reduce heat; cover and simmer for 2½ hours or until hominy is soft. Yield: about 6 cups.

PORK AND MACARONI CASSEROLE

¼ cup chopped onion
2 tablespoons butter or margarine
1 pound pork tenderloin, cubed
1 teaspoon salt
⅛ teaspoon pepper
1½ cups macaroni noodles, uncooked
1 (16-ounce) can whole tomatoes, undrained and coarsely chopped
¾ cup (3 ounces) shredded sharp Cheddar cheese
¼ pound bulk pork sausage, cooked, crumbled, and drained

Sauté onion in butter in a heavy skillet until tender. Add cubed pork, salt, and pepper; cook over medium heat 10 minutes or until pork is browned.

Cook macaroni according to package directions; drain. Combine tenderloin mixture, tomatoes, and macaroni; spoon into a 2-quart casserole. Combine cheese and sausage; sprinkle over top of casserole. Bake, uncovered, at 350° for 8 minutes or until cheese melts. Serve immediately. Yield: 6 servings.

PORK AND APPLE PIE

2 pounds lean boneless pork, cubed
Salt and pepper to taste
1 tablespoon all-purpose flour, browned
½ teaspoon salt
¼ teaspoon pepper
3 medium-size cooking apples, peeled, cored and thinly sliced
1 tablespoon plus 2 teaspoons firmly packed brown sugar
¼ teaspoon ground mace
⅛ teaspoon ground cloves
1 tablespoon butter or margarine
Pastry (recipe follows)
1 egg white

Place pork and water to cover in a large skillet; cook 30 minutes over medium heat. Remove from heat; refrigerate 30 minutes or until fat congeals and rises to surface.

Remove 2 tablespoons fat from water, and place in a small saucepan. Drain pork, and transfer to a lightly greased 9-inch pieplate. Season to taste with salt and pepper. Set aside.

Add flour, ½ teaspoon salt, and ¼ teaspoon pepper to saucepan; cook over medium heat, stirring constantly. Remove from heat, and set aside.

Layer apples over pork in pieplate. Sprinkle with sugar, mace, and cloves; dot with butter. Pour gravy over top.

Roll pastry to ⅛-inch thickness on a lightly floured surface; place over pork mixture in pieplate. Trim edges; seal and flute. Cut slits in top of crust to allow steam to escape. Brush crust with egg white. Bake at 375° for 45 minutes or until golden brown. Yield: one 9-inch pie.

Pastry:

1 cup all-purpose flour
½ teaspoon salt
⅓ cup plus 1 tablespoon shortening
2 to 3 tablespoons cold water

Combine flour and salt; cut in shortening with a pastry blender until mixture resembles coarse meal. Using a fork, stir in enough cold water, 1 tablespoon at a time, to moisten dry ingredients. Shape dough into a ball. Chill. Yield: pastry for one 9-inch pie.

Colorful label from a tomato can dates back to the 1920s.

DIXIE PORK PATTIES

2 large red potatoes, cooked, peeled, and mashed
1 pound ground lean pork
¼ cup chopped onion
1 teaspoon salt
¼ teaspoon pepper
¼ teaspoon rubbed sage
2 eggs, beaten
2 tablespoons milk
Vegetable oil

Combine first 8 ingredients; mix well. Shape into 3-inch patties, about ½-inch thick.

Heat ⅛ inch oil to 375° in a skillet. Fry patties 3 to 5 minutes on each side over medium heat. Drain well. Serve hot. Yield: 16 patties.

Pork Cakes baked in a vegetable sauce pique the appetite.

GREEK CABBAGE ROLLS

1 medium cabbage
½ cup chopped onion
2 cloves garlic, minced
2 tablespoons shortening
¾ pound lean ground pork
¼ pound ground chuck
¼ cup regular rice, uncooked
4 cups boiling water
2 (8-ounce) cans tomato sauce
1 teaspoon salt
½ teaspoon pepper

Core and wash cabbage. Separate leaves, and cook in boiling water 3 minutes or until limp. Drain and set aside.

Sauté onion and garlic in hot shortening in a large skillet until tender. Add meat and rice; cook until meat is browned, stirring to crumble.

Place 2 tablespoons meat mixture in center of each cabbage leaf; fold ends of leaves over, and fasten with wooden picks. Place in a Dutch oven. Add water, tomato sauce, salt, and pepper. Bring to a boil. Reduce heat; cover and simmer 1 to 1½ hours. Remove rolls to a serving platter; serve with sauce. Yield: 8 servings.

EASY SOUTHERN STEW

1¼ pounds lean ground pork
2 medium onions, chopped
1 (14½-ounce) can whole tomatoes, undrained and chopped
1 (10-ounce) package frozen whole kernel corn
¼ cup water
3 tablespoons catsup
1 tablespoon Worcestershire sauce
1 tablespoon sugar
½ teaspoon salt
¼ teaspoon pepper

Cook pork and onion in a large skillet until meat is browned, stirring to crumble. Drain. Stir in remaining ingredients. Bring to a boil. Reduce heat; simmer, uncovered, 20 minutes. Yield: 4 to 6 servings.

PORK CAKES

1½ cups soft breadcrumbs
¾ cup evaporated milk
1½ pounds lean ground pork
⅓ cup finely chopped onion
1½ teaspoons salt
½ teaspoon pepper
2½ tablespoons shortening
¾ cup catsup
¾ cup water
¾ cup finely chopped celery
3 tablespoons prepared horseradish
3 tablespoons lemon juice

Combine breadcrumbs and milk in a medium mixing bowl, stirring well; set aside 5 minutes. Add pork, onion, salt, and pepper; mix well. Shape pork mixture into 12 patties.

Melt shortening in a large skillet over medium heat. Brown patties on both sides; drain well. Place patties in a lightly greased 13- x 9- x 2-inch baking dish.

Combine remaining ingredients; stir well. Pour over patties. Cover; bake at 350° for 50 minutes. Yield: 6 servings.

CAJUN PORK PIE

2 pounds lean ground pork
1 cup chopped celery
½ cup chopped onion
1 clove garlic, crushed
¼ cup chopped fresh parsley
1 teaspoon salt
½ teaspoon pepper
¼ teaspoon dried whole marjoram
⅛ teaspoon ground cloves
⅛ teaspoon ground mace
2 tablespoons all-purpose flour
2 beef-flavored bouillon cubes
1 cup boiling water
Pastry (recipes follows)
1 egg yolk, beaten
Tomato roses (optional)

Combine first 4 ingredients in a Dutch oven; cook over medium heat, stirring occasionally, until pork is browned. Stir in seasonings. Cover; cook over low heat 30 minutes. Drain. Add flour; stir well. Dissolve bouillon cubes in water; add to pork mixture. Cook over medium heat 1 minute; stir constantly. Remove from heat; cool slightly.

Roll half of pastry to ⅛-inch thickness on a lightly floured surface; fit into a 10-inch pieplate. Spoon pork mixture into pastry shell. Roll remaining pastry to ⅛-inch thickness; place over filling. Trim edges; seal and flute. Brush top of crust with beaten yolk. Bake at 400° for 45 minutes or until golden brown. Cut into wedges, and serve hot or cold. Garnish with tomato roses, if desired. Yield: one 10-inch pie.

Pastry:

3 cups all-purpose flour
½ cup shortening
½ cup butter
¾ to 1 cup cold water

Place flour in a mixing bowl; cut in shortening and butter until mixture resembles coarse meal. Sprinkle water over flour mixture; stir with a fork until dry ingredients are moistened. Shape into a ball; chill 30 minutes. Yield: pastry for one double-crust 10-inch pie.

SAVANNAH'S FAMOUS FRIED RICE

3 tablespoons vegetable oil, divided
½ cup chopped green onion
3 cups cooked rice
2 eggs, slightly beaten
2 cups cooked, diced pork
1 (14-ounce) can bean sprouts, drained
1 (8-ounce) can sliced water chestnuts, drained
2 tablespoons soy sauce
1 teaspoon salt

Pour 1 tablespoon oil around top of a preheated wok, coating sides; allow oil to heat to high (375°) for 1 minute. Add onion, and stir-fry until tender. Stir in cooked rice, and heat thoroughly. Push rice mixture up along sides of wok.

Add remaining oil to wok, and reduce heat to low (225°); scramble eggs in oil, and mix in with rice. Add remaining ingredients; mix well. Cover and cook 3 minutes. Serve immediately. Yield: 6 to 8 servings.

PORK HASH

4 cups cooked, cubed pork
2 small onions, chopped
3 tablespoons butter or margarine
4 medium-size red potatoes, peeled and cubed
3 cups water
1 teaspoon salt
1 teaspoon dry mustard
¼ teaspoon pepper
2 tablespoons all-purpose flour
Hot biscuits

Sauté pork and onion in butter in a large Dutch oven over low heat 5 minutes, stirring frequently. Add potatoes, water, salt, mustard, and pepper; simmer, uncovered, 30 minutes or until potatoes are tender.

Combine ¼ cup broth from Dutch oven and flour in a small mixing bowl; stir until smooth. Stir flour mixture into pork and potato broth; cook until thickened. Serve over hot biscuits. Yield: 8 servings.

New York Public Library

Montezuma II

MONTEZUMA PIE

2 medium tomatoes, peeled and quartered
½ cup chopped onion
¾ teaspoon salt
6 flour tortillas
Vegetable oil
2 cups cooked, diced pork
1 (8-ounce) carton commercial sour cream
3 whole green chiles, chopped
2 cups (8 ounces) shredded sharp Cheddar cheese
Hot pepper slices

Place tomatoes in container of an electric blender; process until pureed. Combine tomatoes, onion, and salt in a saucepan; bring to a boil. Reduce heat; simmer 5 minutes or until onion is tender.

Cut tortillas into fourths; fry in ¼ inch hot oil 5 seconds on each side or until softened and lightly browned. Drain well.

Layer one-third of tortillas in a lightly greased 2-quart casserole. Layer half of tomato mixture, diced pork, sour cream, green chiles, and cheese over tortillas. Repeat procedure.

Cover and bake at 350° for 10 minutes. Place remaining tortillas around outside edge of casserole. Bake, uncovered, an additional 10 minutes. Garnish with hot pepper slices. Serve immediately. Yield: 6 servings.

Montezuma Pie combines Mexican tortillas and chiles for a Southwestern taste.

OUTDOOR COOKERY

Barbecue predates the Spaniards' arrival on the South Atlantic coast where they found the Indians cooking meat and fish on racks over open fires. Who knows for how many centuries man had been spitting meat with green sticks or iron rods and then roasting it over coals? No, what is barbecue to us has more to do with the mopping and sopping sauces that developed in the South and westward into Texas and Oklahoma than with the meat itself.

Our sauces differ in color and intensity, from tomato-red to transparent sneaky-hot. Meat runs the gamut from chicken to beef. But, like the time George Washington visited Alexandria, Virginia, and gorged himself for three days on barbecued pork, Southerners want pork — it can be chops, kabobs, or sausage — when they grill or barbecue.

Well, most Southerners want pork. In the arid parts of Texas and Oklahoma, beef emerged as the national dish. Go far enough West and cabrito (goat meat) satisfies best. In western Kentucky, mutton shares the honors with pork at the annual International Bar-B-Q Festival at Owensboro. In Memphis, ribs are the basic pork diet, and they come wet or dry, as ordered. Eastern Tennessee and Kentucky like chicken a lot, but pork is not far behind in the polls.

Where would politics or church fund-raisers be without barbecues? No Kentuckian has ever been elected to a position of consequence without attending the annual rally at Fancy Farm and making a grand show of enjoying the mutton along with the pork.

In Georgia and the coastal states, they chop their pork, agreeing with the Kentuckian who, whacking away at a barbecued shoulder with a giant knife, remarked, "If you can slice it, it ain't done." Some aficionados won't enter a commercial barbecue stand, no matter how fetchingly tacky it looks, without first walking around to view the woodpile. If they find instead a heap of #10 cans, they leave the parking lot in a cloud of dirt and gravel.

Yes, there is fine eating to be had in the unlikeliest looking spots. The trick . . . and the fun . . . is in finding them.

A North Carolina pig pickin' photographed at the John Jones House, New Bern, includes Carolina Brunswick Stew, sliced tomatoes, iced tea, Mustard Cole Slaw, and Old-Fashioned Skillet Cornbread. Good eating!

NORTH CAROLINA PIG PICKIN'

North Carolinians call their big barbecues "pig pickin's" because it is all right (they'll look at you oddly if you don't) to march right up to the tenderly cooked carcass and pick the meat off with your fingers. To fox hunters in these parts, a pig pickin' is both restful and nourishing. But North Carolina is a state divided: On the eastern side, the sauce is a thin vinegar-flavored condiment. To the west, "Lexington-style" sauce is made red with catsup or tomato sauce. Either sauce seeps under the obligatory slaw that goes next on your plate. Add Brunswick Stew (they call it hash in South Carolina), and crowd that plate with hot cornbread.

BARBECUED WHOLE PIG
CAROLINA BRUNSWICK STEW
BOILED NEW POTATOES
MUSTARD COLE SLAW
COLD SLICED TOMATOES
OLD-FASHIONED SKILLET CORNBREAD
SASSO'S BLONDE BROWNIES

Serves 25 to 30

An encampment of Civil War soldiers roasting a pig with makeshift equipment.

BARBECUED WHOLE PIG

1 (75- to 100-pound) dressed pig
½ pound salt
30 pounds charcoal briquets, divided
Barbecue sauce (recipe follows)

Split backbone to allow pig to lay flat, being careful not to pierce skin. Trim and discard any excess fat. Sprinkle salt inside cavity. Set pig aside.

Place 20 pounds charcoal in pork cooker. Pour 1 quart charcoal lighter fluid over top, and ignite. Let burn until charcoal has turned ash-grey. Place heavy gauge wire, about the size of pig, over pork cooker, 13 inches from coals.

Place pig flat, skin side up, on wire surface. Close lid of cooker; cook at 225° for 6 hours, adding additional lighted coals as needed to maintain temperature in cooker.

Place a second piece of wire over pig, sandwiching pig between the 2 layers of wire. Turn pig over; remove wire from top. Insert meat thermometer in thigh; do not touch bone.

Baste meat with barbecue sauce; pour sauce in rib cavity to measure 1 inch. Close pork cooker lid; cook at 225° for 2 hours or until meat thermometer registers 170° and no pink meat is visible when hams and shoulders are cut.

Slice and chop meat or allow guests to pull (pick) meat from bones. Serve with barbecue sauce. Yield: 70 servings.

Note: Meat may be cooked and frozen for up to 3 months.

Barbecue Sauce:

1 gallon vinegar
¾ cup salt
2 tablespoons red pepper
3 tablespoons red pepper flakes
1 cup firmly packed brown sugar or ½ cup molasses

Combine all ingredients; mix well. Allow to stand 4 hours before using. Yield: about 1 gallon.

Split pig is placed on specially built barbecue "pit" between heavy wire mesh, skin side up.

Willis Peaden of Havelock, North Carolina, turns pig, skin side down, halfway through cooking.

The next step is to sauce the pig.

CAROLINA BRUNSWICK STEW

- 2 (3- to 3½-pound) broiler-fryers, cut up
- 1 tablespoon salt, divided
- 5 medium-size red potatoes, peeled and quartered
- 2 (14½-ounce) cans whole tomatoes, undrained and chopped
- 1 small onion, chopped
- 1 teaspoon sugar
- ½ teaspoon pepper
- 2 (10-ounce) packages frozen lima beans
- 3 (10-ounce) packages frozen whole kernel corn

Place chicken, 2 teaspoons salt, and water to cover in a large stockpot. Bring to a boil. Reduce heat; cover and simmer 45 minutes or until chicken is tender. Remove chicken from broth; cool. Reserve broth. Bone chicken, and cut into bite-size pieces. Set aside.

Add potatoes to chicken broth; cook over medium heat 15 minutes or until potatoes are tender. Mash potatoes in broth; add chopped chicken, tomatoes, onion, sugar, remaining salt, and pepper. Cook, uncovered, over medium heat 45 minutes, stirring frequently.

Add lima beans and corn; cook over low heat 20 minutes or until lima beans are tender. Yield: about 7 quarts.

Brunswick stew, cooked in iron vats over open fires: Hearty fare for opening a construction site in Virginia. 1930s photograph.

MUSTARD COLE SLAW

- 2 (3-pound) heads cabbage, shredded
- 4 medium onions, chopped
- 4 medium-size green peppers, chopped
- 2 (4-ounce) jars diced pimiento, drained (optional)
- 2 cups vinegar
- 2 cups sugar
- 2 cups vegetable oil
- 2 tablespoons salt
- 1 tablespoon plus 1 teaspoon celery seeds

Combine shredded cabbage, onion, green pepper, and pimiento, if desired, in a very large bowl; mix well.

Combine remaining ingredients in a mixing bowl, and stir well. Pour vinegar mixture over cabbage mixture, and mix thoroughly. Cover; refrigerate overnight. Yield: 25 to 30 servings.

OLD-FASHIONED SKILLET CORNBREAD

- 6 cups cornmeal
- 3 cups all-purpose flour
- 1 tablespoon baking powder
- 1½ teaspoons salt
- 6 cups buttermilk
- ¼ cup plus 2 tablespoons mayonnaise
- 3 eggs, beaten

Combine cornmeal, flour, baking powder, and salt in a large mixing bowl; mix well. Add buttermilk, mayonnaise, and eggs, mixing well.

Heat three well-greased 9-inch cast-iron skillets in a 400° oven for 3 minutes or until very hot. Divide batter among three skillets. Bake at 425° for 25 minutes or until golden brown. Yield: 25 to 30 servings.

Quite a different form of whole roast pig is cooked in the northern Acadian area of Louisiana, first settled by former soldiers of Napoleon. At one time suckling pig was used; now an animal of 50 to 90 pounds is done *a la broche*. Wrapped in wire mesh, and mounted vertically, head-down, it cooks on an electric spit (broche) before an open fire enclosed on three sides by tin sheeting. The pig cooks about an hour per five pounds of weight. It is turned head-up when three-fourths done.

SASSO'S BLONDE BROWNIES

- 1 cup butter or margarine
- 1 (16-ounce) package light brown sugar
- 2 eggs, beaten
- 2 cups all-purpose flour
- 2 teaspoons baking powder
- Pinch of salt
- 1 cup chopped pecans
- 1 teaspoon vanilla extract

Melt butter in a heavy saucepan over medium heat. Add sugar; mix well. Remove from heat. Stir in eggs, flour, baking powder, and salt. Add pecans and vanilla, mixing well.

Pour batter into a greased 13- x 9- x 2-inch baking pan. Bake at 350° for 30 minutes or until a wooden pick inserted in center comes out clean. Cool and cut into 2-inch squares. Yield: about 2 dozen.

Note: Recipe may be doubled.

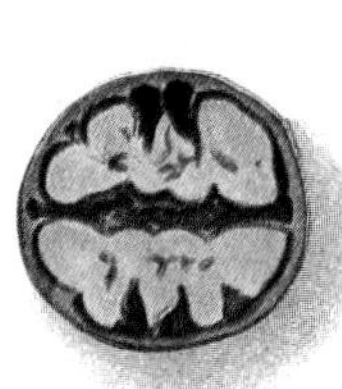

LOUISIANA-STYLE PORK ROAST

1 (6½- to 7-pound) boneless pork loin roast
1 cup soy sauce
1 cup red wine
½ cup cider vinegar
¼ cup lemon juice
½ teaspoon prepared mustard
3 cloves garlic, minced

Place roast in a large plastic bag. Combine remaining ingredients; pour into bag over roast. Fasten bag securely; refrigerate overnight, turning bag occasionally. Remove roast from marinade; reserve marinade.

Insert spit through center of roast; secure with prongs at each end of spit. Balance roast properly to avoid strain on motor. Insert meat thermometer into thickest part of roast, being careful not to touch fat or spit. Place on rotisserie 3 to 4 inches from low coals.

Grill 2½ to 3 hours or until meat thermometer registers 170°. Brush roast with marinade during last hour of grilling. Yield: 16 to 20 servings.

A real show-off at the Hog Show, Monroe County, Alabama, 1948.

A distinction must be made between barbecuing and the spit-roasting done in the fireplaces of our forebears. A colonial woman used a "clear" fire and would have been mortified if her fresh ham had been tinged with smoke. Barbecue is cooked in smoke, which flavors meat and colors it a rich mahogany. The meat is cooked slowly, covered to keep smoke on it; a pork shoulder may take 12 to 24 hours to cook. In grilling, the meat is seared and then finished at a lower temperature.

SPIT-ROASTED PORK LOIN ROAST

1 cup catsup
½ cup water
¼ cup vegetable oil
¼ cup red wine vinegar
2 tablespoons Worcestershire sauce
2 tablespoons instant minced onion
1 tablespoon firmly packed brown sugar
1 teaspoon mustard seeds
1 teaspoon dried whole oregano
½ teaspoon salt
½ teaspoon cracked black pepper
¼ teaspoon chili powder
1 bay leaf
1 (5- to 5½-pound) pork loin roast, rolled and tied

Combine first 13 ingredients in a medium saucepan. Cook mixture, uncovered, over low heat, 20 minutes, stirring occasionally. Remove bay leaf, and discard.

Thread roast on a spit; secure tightly with prongs at each end of spit. Make sure roast is properly balanced to avoid strain on motor when spit is turning. Insert meat thermometer into thickest part of roast, being careful not to touch fat or spit. Place spit on rotisserie 4 to 6 inches from medium coals. Grill roast 4 hours or until meat thermometer registers 170°, basting frequently with sauce during last 30 minutes. Remove roast from spit; allow to stand 15 to 20 minutes before slicing. Yield: 10 to 12 servings.

ORANGE-BASTED PORK ROAST

1 (4½- to 5-pound) pork shoulder roast
Garlic salt
Baked Orange Glaze

Sprinkle roast with garlic salt. Insert meat thermometer, being careful not to touch bone or fat. Grill 6 to 8 inches from hot coals for 3½ hours or until meat thermometer registers 170°. During last 30 minutes of grilling time, turn and baste frequently with Baked Orange Glaze. Let stand 20 to 25 minutes before carving. Serve with glaze. Yield: 6 to 8 servings.

Baked Orange Glaze:

3 medium oranges, unpeeled
1 cup sugar
1 cup water
¼ cup plus 2 tablespoons light corn syrup

Place oranges in a medium saucepan; cover with water. Bring to a boil, and boil 30 minutes. Drain; let oranges cool to room temperature and quarter.

Combine remaining ingredients in a medium saucepan; stir well, and boil 5 minutes.

Place orange quarters in an 8-inch square pan. Pour sugar mixture over orange quarters; place pan on grill 6 to 8 inches from hot coals. Cook 1½ hours, basting oranges with syrup occasionally. Use for basting pork. Yield: 2 cups.

BARBECUED LEG OF PORK

1 (14- to 16-pound) leg of pork (fresh ham)
Hot Barbecue Sauce

Insert meat thermometer into ham, being careful not to touch bone or fat. Place meat on grill 8 inches from hot coals. Cover and cook 4½ hours, turning occasionally. Uncover and baste with Hot Barbecue Sauce. Cover and cook an additional 2 hours or until meat thermometer registers 170°; baste frequently with sauce.

Let meat stand 20 minutes; slice and serve with remaining sauce. Yield: 20 to 25 servings.

Hot Barbecue Sauce:

1 (24-ounce) bottle catsup
2 cups vinegar
3 tablespoons pepper
2 tablespoons salt
2 tablespoons paprika
1 tablespoon chili powder
1 tablespoon hot sauce
1 tablespoon Worcestershire sauce
¾ teaspoon dry mustard

Combine all ingredients in a medium mixing bowl, stirring until well blended. Yield: about 5 cups.

Barbecued Leg of Pork is worth every minute of the time it takes to cook in the covered grill.

Dr. M.W. Sharp, copy courtesy of the Institute of Texan Cultures

All the fixings come together for a barbecue at Castroville, Texas, photographed c.1900.

SMOKED PORK SHOULDER

1 quart vinegar
⅛ pound dried whole red peppers, seeded and chopped
Juice of 1 lemon
1 teaspoon salt
½ teaspoon pepper
1 (4- to 4½-pound) pork shoulder roast

Combine first 5 ingredients in a large saucepan; bring mixture to a boil. Reduce heat; simmer, uncovered, 10 minutes. Set sauce aside.

Prepare charcoal fire in smoker, and let burn 10 to 15 minutes. Place water pan in smoker; fill with ¼ cup sauce and 1 quart water.

Trim skin from roast. Place roast on food rack, and baste generously on all sides with sauce. Insert meat thermometer, being careful not to touch bone or fat.

Cover with smoker lid; cook 9 to 11 hours or until meat thermometer registers 170°, basting frequently with sauce after 6 hours. Refill water pan with additional sauce as needed. To serve, thinly slice roast. Yield: 8 to 10 servings.

Note: Remaining sauce may be refrigerated and reheated for basting other meats.

SLICED BARBECUED PORK

4 cups catsup
2 cups vinegar
2 tablespoons plus ¼ teaspoon lemon juice
1 tablespoon hot sauce
1½ teaspoons Worcestershire sauce
½ teaspoon olive oil
½ teaspoon prepared mustard
¼ teaspoon garlic salt
½ cup cider vinegar
¾ teaspoon hot sauce
1 (5- to 5½-pound) pork shoulder roast

Combine catsup, 2 cups vinegar, lemon juice, 1 tablespoon hot sauce, Worcestershire sauce, olive oil, mustard, and garlic salt in a small Dutch oven; stir well. Cook, uncovered, over low heat 1 hour, stirring occasionally.

Combine ½ cup cider vinegar and ¾ teaspoon hot sauce; stir well. Set aside.

Place roast 6 to 8 inches from slow coals. Insert meat thermometer, being careful not to touch bone or fat. Grill 6 to 7 hours or until meat thermometer registers 170°, turning frequently and basting frequently with vinegar-hot sauce mixture. Baste meat with barbecue sauce during last hour of grilling.

Slice meat thinly, and toss with enough barbecue sauce to coat well. Remaining barbecue sauce may be kept refrigerated for other uses. Yield: 6 servings.

BARBECUE SPECIALTIES

GRILLED PORK CHOPS

¼ cup lemon juice
¼ cup butter or margarine
2 tablespoons Worcestershire sauce
¼ teaspoon salt
¼ teaspoon pepper
4 (1-inch-thick) pork chops

Combine first 5 ingredients in a small saucepan, and mix well. Bring mixture to a boil. Reduce heat; simmer, uncovered, 15 minutes. Set aside.

Place pork chops on grill 5 inches from hot coals; grill 20 to 25 minutes on each side, basting frequently with sauce. Yield: 4 servings.

HICKORY-SMOKED STUFFED PORK CHOPS

½ cup chopped onion
½ cup chopped celery
¼ cup butter or margarine
1 cup herb-seasoned dressing
⅓ cup water
¼ teaspoon salt
¼ teaspoon pepper
4 (1½-inch-thick) pork loin chops, cut with pockets
Hickory chips, soaked in water
Liquid smoke

Sauté onion and celery in butter in a medium saucepan until tender. Stir in dressing, water, salt, and pepper. Remove from heat. Spoon mixture into pockets of pork chops, and secure with wooden picks.

Place coals to one side of covered grill; when coals are grey-white, sprinkle with hickory chips. Place chops on opposite side of grill from coals for indirect cooking; cover grill. Cook chops 1 hour or until well done, turning chops and sprinkling with liquid smoke every 15 minutes. Yield: 4 servings.

HONEY PORK CHOPS

4 (¾-inch-thick) pork chops
1 teaspoon lemon-pepper seasoning
½ cup plus 1 tablespoon lemon juice
2 tablespoons honey
¼ teaspoon salt

Sprinkle pork chops lightly with lemon-pepper seasoning. Place in a shallow baking dish; pour lemon juice over chops. Cover and marinate in refrigerator at least 2 hours, turning chops every 30 minutes.

Remove chops from marinade, and place 5 to 6 inches from slow to medium coals; grill 20 to 25 minutes, turning frequently. About 5 minutes before removing chops from grill, lightly brush each side with honey, and sprinkle with salt. Yield: 4 servings.

If fed this feed, surely prosperity and health will follow.

Collection of Business Americana

BARBECUED PORK CHOPS

1½ cups water
¾ cup catsup
¾ cup vinegar
1 medium onion, chopped
1 clove garlic, minced
1 tablespoon Worcestershire sauce
3 tablespoons firmly packed brown sugar
2 teaspoons salt
½ teaspoon pepper
¼ teaspoon hot sauce
8 (1¼-inch-thick) pork loin chops (about 4½ pounds)

Combine first 10 ingredients in a small saucepan. Bring to a boil. Reduce heat; cook, uncovered, 30 minutes over low heat, stirring occasionally.

Place chops 4 to 5 inches from medium coals; grill 15 minutes on each side, basting frequently with sauce. Serve any remaining sauce with chops. Yield: 8 servings.

COUNTRY-PRIDE PORK CHOPS

½ cup soy sauce
¼ cup sherry
¼ firmly packed brown sugar
1 teaspoon ground cinnamon
½ teaspoon garlic salt
Dash of ground ginger
4 (1-inch-thick) center-cut pork chops

Combine first 6 ingredients, mixing well; pour into a shallow baking dish. Add pork chops; cover and marinate in refrigerator overnight, turning chops several times.

Remove chops from marinade, reserving marinade for basting. Place chops 6 inches from medium coals; grill 15 minutes on each side, basting frequently with reserved marinade. Yield: 4 servings.

MARINATED PORK STEAKS

1 (8¼-ounce) can pineapple slices, undrained
1 medium onion, chopped
½ cup soy sauce
¼ cup vegetable oil
3 tablespoons light corn syrup
1 teaspoon ground ginger
4 (¾-inch-thick) pork blade steaks

Drain pineapple, reserving syrup for sauce; set pineapple slices aside.

Combine pineapple syrup, onion, soy sauce, oil, syrup, and ginger in a small saucepan. Cook, uncovered, over medium heat 10 minutes, stirring frequently.

Place meat in a shallow baking dish, and cover with marinade; cover and refrigerate overnight.

Remove pork steaks from marinade, reserving marinade for basting. Place steaks 4 to 6 inches from slow to medium coals. Grill 35 minutes or until steaks are no longer pink, turning and basting occasionally with reserved marinade. Place reserved pineapple slices on grill, and grill 1 minute on each side. Garnish pork steaks with grilled pineapple slices. Yield: 4 servings.

Marinated Pork Steaks with the faintly Oriental flavor of ginger and soy sauce are complemented by slices of grilled pineapple.

Pig is weighed at H.C. Wood's farm, Craven County, North Carolina, 1929.

BARBECUED HAM STEAKS

¼ cup plus 1 tablespoon firmly packed brown sugar
1 tablespoon dry mustard
1 teaspoon onion salt
1 cup unsweetened pineapple juice
2 tablespoons lemon juice
2 teaspoons soy sauce
1 (8¼-ounce) can sliced pineapple, drained
2 (½-inch-thick) slices smoked ham (about ¾ pound)

Combine first 6 ingredients in a heavy saucepan, stirring well. Bring mixture to a boil. Reduce heat; simmer, uncovered, 5 minutes. Stir frequently. Remove from heat.

Place ham steaks 3 to 4 inches from medium coals. Grill slowly 20 to 25 minutes, basting and turning every 5 minutes. Place pineapple slices on grill; grill 1 minute on each side or until just heated. Garnish ham steaks with grilled pineapple rings, and serve with remaining sauce. Yield: 4 servings.

SOUTHERN BARBECUED SPARERIBS

2 cloves garlic, minced
2 tablespoons butter or margarine
1 cup catsup
¾ cup chili sauce
¼ cup firmly packed brown sugar
2 tablespoons prepared mustard
2 tablespoons Worcestershire sauce
1 tablespoon celery seeds
2 dashes hot sauce
½ teaspoon salt
1½ cups water
4 pounds pork spareribs, cut into 4 serving-size pieces

Sauté garlic in butter in a heavy saucepan. Stir in catsup, chili sauce, sugar, mustard, Worcestershire sauce, celery seeds, hot sauce, salt, and water. Bring to a boil. Remove from heat, and set aside.

Place spareribs and water to cover in a large Dutch oven. Bring to a boil. Reduce heat; cover and simmer 45 minutes or until tender. Drain well.

Place ribs, bone side down, on grill over slow coals. Grill 10 minutes; turn meaty side down, and cook 10 minutes. Cook 10 to 15 additional minutes, turning and basting often with sauce. Yield: 4 servings.

Liquid smoke is an ingredient many people mix into their barbecue sauce. It had its commercial beginnings in 1895, but a form of it had been used earlier by no less a personage than Confederate General Thomas J. Jackson who "stood like a stone wall" in the Battle of Bull Run. He noted that water poured on burned wood tasted smoky, and had his men put it on some pork they were barbecuing. Next to General R.E. Lee, "Stonewall" Jackson was the South's most brilliant strategist.

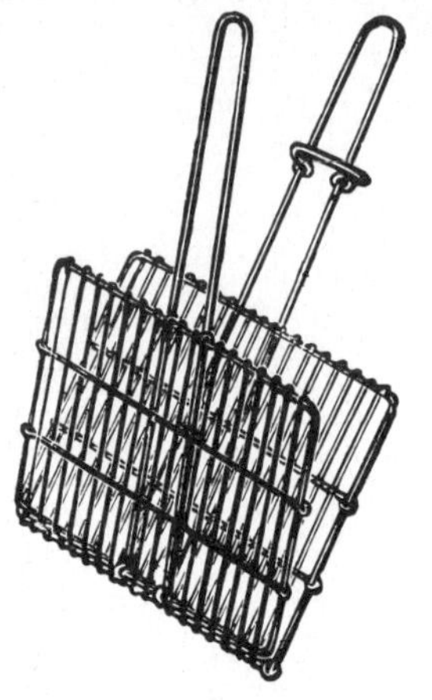

Sometimes [the pig] is basted during these long hours with a wonderful mixture of condiments called a 'soption'; sometimes there's nothing but his own savory juices dripping down onto the coals with a hiss and a little dance of flame. As he slowly turns throughout the impatient hours, a heavenly aroma compounded of roasting pork and wood smoke permeates the atmosphere, announcing as nothing else could that the barbecue is underway.

Duncan Hines' *Food Odyssey*

TEXAS SPARERIBS

3½ to 4 pounds pork spareribs, cut into 4 serving-size pieces
2 teaspoons sugar
2 teaspoons salt
2 teaspoons pepper
Barbecue sauce (recipe follows)

Combine ribs and water to cover in a large Dutch oven. Bring to a boil. Reduce heat; cover and simmer 45 minutes or until tender. Drain.

Combine sugar, salt, and pepper; rub over entire surface of ribs. Place ribs, bone side down, on grill over slow coals. Grill 20 minutes; turn meaty side down, and cook 10 to 15 minutes, basting frequently with barbecue sauce. Yield: 4 servings.

Barbecue Sauce:

¼ cup butter or margarine
1 cup catsup
¼ cup firmly packed brown sugar
2 tablespoons vegetable oil
2 tablespoons Worcestershire sauce
1 tablespoon vinegar
1 tablespoon prepared mustard
⅛ teaspoon pepper
⅛ teaspoon chili powder
Dash of garlic salt
Dash of red pepper

Melt butter in a heavy saucepan. Add remaining ingredients, stirring well. Bring to a boil. Remove from heat. Yield: about 1⅔ cups.

HICKORY-SMOKED PORK RIBS

Hickory chips, soaked in water
4 pounds pork spareribs
Barbecue sauce (recipe follows)

Prepare charcoal fire in smoker, and let burn 10 to 15 minutes. Sprinkle wet hickory chips over grey-white coals. Place water pan in smoker, and fill with hot water.

Place lower food rack on appropriate shelf in smoker. Place ribs on shelf; cover with smoker lid, and cook about 3½ hours. Remove lid, and baste ribs with barbecue sauce during last 5 minutes of cooking; replace lid immediately after basting. Serve remaining sauce with ribs. Yield: 4 servings.

Barbecue Sauce:

1 medium onion, chopped
2 tablespoons vegetable oil
1 quart catsup
1 cup prepared mustard
¼ cup sugar
¼ cup Worcestershire sauce
2 teaspoons lemon juice
1½ teaspoons vinegar
1 small clove garlic, minced
1½ teaspoons pepper
½ teaspoon salt
Hot sauce

Sauté onion in oil in a large saucepan until tender. Add remaining ingredients, and stir well. Simmer, uncovered, 15 minutes or until thickened. Yield: 4¾ cups.

COUNTRY-STYLE RIBS

3 to 4 pounds country-style ribs, cut into 6 serving-size pieces
1 onion, peeled and sliced
¼ cup finely chopped onion
1 clove garlic, minced
3 tablespoons butter or margarine
1 cup catsup
½ cup cider vinegar
2 tablespoons Worcestershire sauce
1 tablespoon sugar
2 teaspoons prepared mustard
½ teaspoon salt
¼ teaspoon pepper
Juice of ½ lemon

Combine ribs, sliced onion, and water to cover in a large Dutch oven. Bring to a boil. Reduce heat; cover and simmer 45 minutes or until ribs are tender. Drain and set aside.

Sauté chopped onion and garlic in butter in a medium saucepan until tender. Stir in catsup, vinegar, Worcestershire sauce, sugar, mustard, salt, pepper, and lemon juice. Bring to a boil. Remove from heat.

Place ribs on grill 4 to 6 inches from medium coals. Cook 20 to 30 minutes, turning and basting frequently with sauce. Yield: 6 servings.

Country-Style Ribs (front) are parboiled before grilling. Hickory-Smoked Pork Ribs are cooked in a covered barbecue smoker.

Allen Chesney, *Chattanooga Album*, University of Tennessee Press, Knoxville

Busy Bee Barbecue in Chattanooga, Tennessee, 1926.

GRILLED SWEET-AND-SOUR SPARERIBS

2 tablespoons butter or margarine
1 medium onion, chopped
1 (16-ounce) can pitted purple plums, undrained
1 (6-ounce) can frozen lemonade concentrate, thawed and undiluted
¼ cup chili sauce
¼ cup soy sauce
2 tablespoons salt, divided
2 teaspoons prepared mustard
1 teaspoon Worcestershire sauce
1 teaspoon ground ginger
2 drops hot sauce
8 to 8½ pounds spareribs

Melt butter in a medium saucepan over low heat; add onion, and cook until tender.

Place plums and plum juice in container of an electric blender; process until smooth. Add pureed plums to onion. Stir in lemonade, chili sauce, soy sauce, 1 tablespoon salt, mustard, Worcestershire sauce, ginger, and hot sauce. Cook, uncovered, over low heat 15 minutes, stirring occasionally. Remove from heat; set aside to cool. Cover and refrigerate sauce overnight.

Cut ribs into serving-size pieces (3 to 4 ribs per person). Place ribs, 1 tablespoon salt, and water to cover in a large stockpot. Bring to a boil; cover and simmer over medium heat 45 minutes or until ribs are tender. Drain well.

Place ribs, bone side down, on grill over slow coals. Grill 10 minutes; turn meaty side down, and cook until browned. Brush sweet-and-sour sauce on both sides of the ribs, and cook 5 minutes on each side. Serve any remaining sauce with ribs. Yield: 8 servings.

MARINATED SMOKED SPARERIBS

1 teaspoon salt
¼ teaspoon sugar
⅛ teaspoon ground turmeric
⅛ teaspoon paprika
⅛ teaspoon celery salt
⅛ teaspoon pepper
3 pounds pork spareribs, cut into 4 serving-size pieces
1 cup catsup
¾ cup water
½ cup chopped green pepper
½ cup chopped onion
⅓ cup cider vinegar
¼ cup firmly packed dark brown sugar
1 tablespoon Worcestershire sauce
1 teaspoon dry mustard
½ teaspoon hot sauce
½ teaspoon salt
¼ teaspoon pepper
¼ teaspoon dried whole basil
2 cloves garlic, minced

Combine first 6 ingredients; rub over entire surface of ribs.

Combine remaining ingredients in a large shallow pan. Place ribs in marinade; cover and refrigerate overnight.

Place spareribs on grill of smoker. Pour remaining marinade over spareribs into water pan. Cover and smoke 5 to 6 hours. Yield: 4 servings.

Mustard can, early 1900s.

Collection of Business Americana

Half the fun of a horseback outing is open-fire cookery. Smoky Mountains, 1940.

FLORIDA BARBECUED COUNTRY-STYLE RIBS

¼ cup vegetable oil, divided
1 small onion, chopped
1 clove garlic, minced
1 (6-ounce) can tomato paste
¾ cup water
½ cup vinegar
2 tablespoons sugar
1 tablespoon Worcestershire sauce
1½ teaspoons salt
1 teaspoon dry mustard
⅛ teaspoon pepper
⅛ teaspoon chili powder
4 whole cloves
1 bay leaf
3 drops hot sauce
5 pounds country-style pork ribs, cut into 6 serving-size pieces
1 tablespoon salt

Heat 1 tablespoon oil in a medium saucepan; add onion and garlic. Cook over low heat until onion is tender.

Add next 12 ingredients, stirring well. Bring mixture to a boil. Reduce heat; cover and simmer 1 hour. Remove whole cloves and bay leaf; discard. Set sauce aside.

Place ribs, 1 tablespoon salt, and water to cover in a large Dutch oven. Bring to a boil. Reduce heat; cover and simmer 30 minutes or until ribs are tender. Drain.

Place ribs on grill over slow coals. Grill 5 minutes on each side. Brush both sides of meat liberally with sauce; grill an additional 5 minutes on each side. Serve remaining sauce with ribs. Yield: 6 servings.

An account of an 1859 Florida barbecue goes like this: "Ever so many deep pits had been dug and all night fires had been burning in these pits, fires made of oakwood (for pine would spoil the taste). Over these pits of glowing coals green hickory saplings had been placed . . . whole beeves, many of them; whole hogs, I dare not say how many. It takes a lot to feed so many strong healthy appetites. Later in the day bread would be baked, potatoes roasted, coffee made.

SOUTHERN TENDER KABOBS

½ cup soy sauce
¼ cup firmly packed brown sugar
2 tablespoons sherry
½ teaspoon garlic powder
½ teaspoon ground cinnamon
2½ to 3 pounds lean boneless pork, cut into 1½-inch cubes
2 small tomatoes, quartered
2 small onions, peeled and quartered
1 medium-size green pepper, cut into 1-inch pieces
½ pound fresh mushrooms
1 (12-ounce) jar currant jelly
1 tablespoon prepared mustard

Combine soy sauce, brown sugar, sherry, garlic powder, and cinnamon in a large shallow container. Add pork; cover and marinate in refrigerator 4 hours or overnight.

Remove pork from marinade. Reserve any remaining marinade for other uses. Place pork on skewers. Alternate vegetables on skewers. Set vegetable kabobs aside.

Combine jelly and mustard in a small saucepan; bring to a boil, stirring until jelly dissolves. Remove from heat, and set aside.

Grill pork kabobs 20 minutes over medium coals, turning frequently. Place vegetable kabobs on grill. Grill vegetable and pork kabobs 10 to 15 minutes, turning and basting often with jelly sauce. Yield: 6 servings.

Southern Tender Kabobs to grill for a summer's evening.

PORK KABOBS

½ cup olive oil
¼ cup red wine vinegar
2 tablespoons soy sauce
2 cloves garlic, minced
1 teaspoon dry mustard
½ teaspoon celery seeds
½ teaspoon dried whole rosemary
½ teaspoon rubbed sage
Dash of pepper
2 pounds lean boneless pork, cut into 1-inch cubes

Combine all ingredients except pork; mix well. Add pork, and stir to coat; cover and refrigerate overnight. Place pork on skewers; reserve any remaining marinade.

Place kabobs 5 to 6 inches from medium coals. Grill 40 minutes or until done, turning frequently; baste with reserved marinade during last 10 minutes. Serve immediately. Yield: 4 to 6 servings.

MIXED GRILL

1 (16-ounce) package knockwurst
1 (12-ounce) package Polish sausage, cut into 3-inch pieces
8 frankfurters
Mustard Sauce

Place sausages and frankfurters 5 to 6 inches from medium coals. Grill 20 minutes, turning frequently. Serve with Mustard Sauce. Yield: 8 servings.

Mustard Sauce:

1 cup half-and-half
½ cup sugar
½ cup vinegar
1 egg yolk, well beaten
2 tablespoons dry mustard
1 tablespoon all-purpose flour
⅛ teaspoon salt

Combine all ingredients in top of a double boiler; beat with a wire whisk until blended. Cook over warm water, stirring constantly, 1 hour or until slightly thickened. Serve warm or cold. Yield: 2 cups.

Courtesy of Louis Wilhite

Seven people keep up with 1920s machine stuffing sausage at ten feet per second!

GRILLED POLISH SAUSAGE AND CABBAGE

- 6 slices bacon, cut into 1-inch pieces
- ½ cup chopped onion
- ¼ cup sugar
- 2 tablespoons all-purpose flour
- 1½ teaspoons salt
- ⅛ teaspoon pepper
- ⅓ cup vinegar
- ¼ cup water
- 1 medium cabbage, shredded
- 1½ pounds smoked Polish sausage, cut into 3-inch pieces
- 1 pound smoked sausage links

Cook bacon in a large Dutch oven on grill over medium coals until browned and crisp. Drain on paper towels, reserving 2 tablespoons drippings in pan. Set bacon aside.

Sauté onion in drippings until tender. Add sugar, flour, salt, and pepper; stir well. Gradually add vinegar and water; cook over medium coals, stirring constantly, until thickened and bubbly. Stir in cabbage. Cover; cook 15 to 20 minutes, stirring occasionally.

Place sausage on grill 3 inches from medium coals. Grill 15 minutes, turning as needed. Sprinkle bacon over cabbage, and serve with sausage. Yield: 6 servings.

Pork's subtle flavor goes so naturally with a variety of fruits and vegetables that it has become a popular choice for the grill. For pork kabobs, slow gentle heat is the rule, quite different from the approach we take to beef. Polish sausage, bratwurst, knockwurst . . . all the fully cooked and cured sausages . . . take well to the grill too, and cook in a flash. These make a satisfying meal when served with cabbage or sauerkraut.

BARBECUE SAUCES

TEXAS BASTING SAUCE

2 cups butter or margarine, melted
1 cup vegetable oil
½ cup vinegar
½ cup dried parsley flakes
⅓ cup lemon juice
3 tablespoons catsup
1 tablespoon Worcestershire sauce
1 tablespoon chili powder
½ teaspoon salt
¼ teaspoon pepper

Combine all ingredients in a medium saucepan; cook, uncovered, over medium heat 5 minutes, stirring occasionally. Keep sauce warm while basting pork. Yield: 3½ cups.

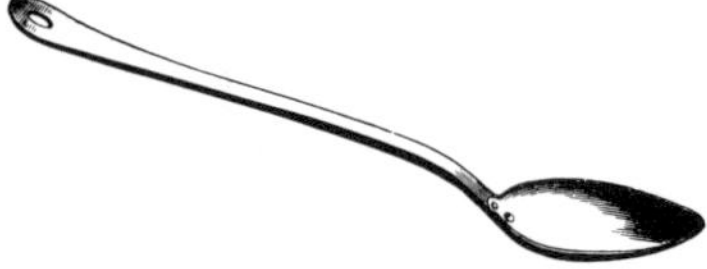

TENNESSEE BASTING SAUCE

3 cups vinegar
1 cup Worcestershire sauce
¼ cup dry mustard
1 tablespoon salt
10 bay leaves
16 whole cloves
1 teaspoon dried whole oregano
1 teaspoon dried whole rosemary
½ teaspoon pepper
¼ teaspoon red pepper
5 cloves garlic
1 lemon, quartered
1 medium onion, quartered
¼ cup butter or margarine
¼ cup catsup
¼ teaspoon hot sauce

Combine all ingredients in a medium Dutch oven; bring to a boil. Reduce heat; simmer, uncovered, 15 minutes. Strain basting sauce, discarding bay leaves, cloves, garlic, lemon, and onion. Use sauce to baste pork during barbecue procedure. Yield: 4 cups.

CAROLINA BASTING SAUCE

1 cup molasses
1 cup prepared mustard
1 cup vinegar

Combine molasses and mustard; mix well. Add vinegar, stirring until well blended. Cover and refrigerate until ready to use. Use as a basting sauce for pork. Yield: 3 cups.

BEER SAUCE FOR BARBECUE

1 small onion, chopped
½ cup butter or margarine
1½ cups vinegar
2½ tablespoons Worcestershire sauce
Grated rind and juice of 2 lemons
1 clove garlic, minced
¾ cup beer

Sauté onion in butter in a medium saucepan until tender. Add vinegar, Worcestershire sauce, lemon rind and juice, and garlic; stir well. Bring to a boil. Reduce heat; simmer, uncovered, 15 minutes. Remove from heat; add beer, stirring well. Use sauce to baste pork during barbecue procedure. Yield: 3 cups.

MOLASSES BARBECUE SAUCE

⅓ cup cider vinegar
⅓ cup prepared mustard
⅓ cup molasses
½ cup chopped onion
Grated rind and juice of 2 lemons
1 teaspoon hot sauce
½ teaspoon salt
½ teaspoon garlic powder
¼ teaspoon pepper

Combine all ingredients in a small saucepan; bring to a boil. Reduce heat; simmer, uncovered, 5 minutes. Serve with pork chops. Yield: 1¼ cups.

HORSERADISH BARBECUE SAUCE

1 medium onion, chopped
1 cup water
1 cup catsup
½ cup vinegar
1 tablespoon chopped fresh parsley
1 tablespoon prepared horseradish
1 tablespoon prepared mustard
1 tablespoon firmly packed brown sugar
1 teaspoon pepper

Combine all ingredients in a medium saucepan; stir well. Bring to a boil. Reduce heat; simmer, uncovered, 10 to 15 minutes, stirring occasionally. Serve sauce with pork roasts. Yield: 3 cups.

LOW COUNTRY BARBECUE SAUCE

1 medium onion, finely chopped
¼ cup butter or margarine
2 cups chopped tomatoes, processed through food mill
¼ cup vinegar
1 tablespoon sugar
1 tablespoon paprika
1 tablespoon pepper
2 teaspoons salt
1½ teaspoons Worcestershire sauce
¼ teaspoon hot sauce
1 clove garlic
½ pod red pepper

Sauté onion in butter in a medium saucepan until tender. Stir in remaining ingredients; bring to a boil. Reduce heat; simmer, uncovered, 15 minutes. Remove and discard garlic and red pepper pod. Serve over sliced pork. Yield: 2 cups.

Front to back: Molasses Barbecue Sauce, Horseradish Barbecue Sauce, and Tennessee Basting Sauce.

HAMS, SMOKED AND CURED

In shopping for ham, we find many forms of the porker's hind legs, so unless we want a fresh roast, we must decide upon a specific kind of cured ham. Curing is accomplished by the addition of salt and potassium nitrate (saltpeter) or nitrite. These chemicals are essential to meat preservation and account for some of the characteristic flavor and color. Meat may be cured wet or dry.

Most famous of the dry cures is the "Genuine Smithfield." The process begins like "Virginia-style" or country ham in any other state, by rubbing the hams with the salt mix and then allowing the meat to form a brine with its own liquid. The Smithfield ham is then dried off, smoked, and hung up to age for at least six months.

Country ham does not have to be smoked, but aging is necessary. Many Southerners insist that smoking adds needed color and flavor; others would skip the smoke taste and opt for ham that has taken salt and then simply been aged. "Genuine Smithfield" hams are usually long-shanked and have been cured, treated, smoked, and processed by law in Smithfield, Virginia.

As dry curing removes moisture from a ham, soaking is necessary to rehydrate it and reduce the salt content. Some cooks use 24 hours of soaking per year's aging as a rule of thumb, up to 48 hours for a two-year-old ham. Even knowing that Southern elegance is best displayed by serving aged, dry-cured ham, we have occasions that simply do not warrant the outlay. For a patio or poolside party of the ham-and-potato-salad variety, we settle for a wet-cured ham.

"Smoked" products cannot weigh more after curing than when fresh. Cured "water-added" hams and shoulders may contain 10 percent more water than before curing, a feat accomplished by pumping in (usually smoke-flavored) liquid. "Imitation hams" contain more than 10 percent of their original weight in water. Cooking methods are on the packages, but it is worth noting that even a "ready to eat" ham is improved by some cooking. Once the ham is purchased, be it a whole, half, or slice, country or "city," cooking begins, and cooking is what makes ham so good.

Fried Country Ham with Red-Eye Gravy, Fried Eggs, and Buttermilk Biscuits: The ultimate Southern breakfast shown at Owens Spring Creek Farm, Richardson, Texas.

COUNTRY HAM BREAKFAST

It has been said that a Southerner who has been raised right never really feels at home in another part of the world. With good reason: Along with his dogwood in spring and his magnolia in summer, he must have country ham every so often. A loyal expatriate, as a rule, treasures his mail-order source of "old ham" from his home state. A Virginian sojourning in New York or a Kentuckian in San Francisco will frost mint juleps and fry precious ham slices for his best new-found friends, nearly always with a tear in his eye. Red-eye gravy is a natural by-product of ham requiring twice as many biscuits as normal. This is, after all, the Southern breakfast of breakfasts.

FRIED COUNTRY HAM
WITH RED-EYE GRAVY
FRIED EGGS
BAKED GRITS
FRIED APPLES
BUTTERMILK BISCUITS
HONEY BUTTER
ASSORTED JELLIES

Serves 8

FRIED COUNTRY HAM WITH RED-EYE GRAVY

4 (¼-inch-thick) slices country ham, about 1½ pounds
1 cup water
¼ cup coffee

Soak ham in cold water to cover for 1 hour; drain ham well and pat dry between paper towels.

Slice ham in half crosswise. Place half of ham slices in an ungreased cast-iron skillet; cook slices over low heat until browned, turning occasionally. Drain well on paper towels. Place ham slices on a large serving platter; keep warm. Repeat procedure with remaining ham slices.

Reserve pan drippings in skillet. Add water and coffee to drippings in skillet. Bring to a boil; remove gravy from heat. Serve red-eye gravy with fried country ham. Yield: 8 servings.

Monitor Windmill ad promises prosperity. Late 1900s.

Collection of Business Americana

Fried Apples. Could anything be better with country ham?

FRIED EGGS

2 tablespoons vegetable oil
8 eggs
Salt and pepper to taste

Heat oil in a heavy skillet until hot enough to sizzle a drop of water. Break each egg into a saucer; carefully slip each egg, one at a time, into skillet. Reduce heat, and cook until whites are firm and yolks are soft, or cook to desired degree of doneness. Season eggs with salt and pepper to taste before serving. Yield: 8 servings.

BAKED GRITS

1½ cups regular grits, uncooked
3 cups water
1 cup evaporated milk
¼ cup butter or margarine, melted
2 eggs, beaten
1 teaspoon salt
1 teaspoon baking powder

Combine grits and water in a heavy saucepan. Bring to a boil; reduce heat, and simmer 2 to 3 minutes. Remove from heat.

Stir in remaining ingredients, mixing well. Pour mixture into a greased 2-quart casserole. Bake at 425° for 25 minutes. Serve immediately. Yield: 8 servings.

FRIED APPLES

3 tablespoons butter
5 large cooking apples, cored, and cut into ½-inch-thick slices
⅔ cup sugar
Ground cinnamon

Melt butter in a large skillet; add a few apple slices at a time. Sprinkle apple slices lightly with sugar. Cover and cook 5 minutes or until apples are tender. Remove apples to a warm serving platter, and sprinkle with cinnamon. Repeat procedure with remaining apple rings. Serve warm. Yield: 8 servings.

BUTTERMILK BISCUITS

2 cups all-purpose flour
1 tablespoon baking powder
¼ teaspoon salt
¼ teaspoon sugar
½ cup shortening
½ teaspoon baking soda
¾ cup buttermilk

Combine first 4 ingredients in a large mixing bowl; mix well. Cut in shortening with a pastry blender until mixture resembles coarse meal.

Dissolve soda in buttermilk. Sprinkle buttermilk mixture evenly over flour mixture, stirring until dry ingredients are moistened. Turn dough out onto a lightly floured surface; knead lightly 2 to 3 times.

Pat dough to ¼-inch thickness; cut biscuits with a 2-inch biscuit cutter. Place in 2 lightly greased 8-inch round cakepans. Bake at 450° for 10 minutes or until lightly browned. Yield: about 1½ dozen.

HONEY BUTTER

1 cup butter, softened
3 tablespoons honey

Cream butter in a small mixing bowl; gradually add honey, beating until smooth. Serve with Buttermilk Biscuits. Yield: about 1 cup.

COUNTRY HAM AND "CITY" COOKING

SYKES INN SMITHFIELD HAM

1 (15-pound) country ham

Place ham in a very large container; cover with cold water. Soak ham overnight. Pour off water, and scrub ham thoroughly with a stiff brush. Rinse.

Place ham and water to cover in a large Dutch oven. Bring to a boil; reduce heat. Cover; simmer 4½ to 5 hours.

Remove ham, and set aside to cool. Discard skin from ham. Place ham, fat side up, in a shallow roasting pan. Score fat in a diamond pattern. Bake at 350° for 30 minutes or until lightly browned. Remove from oven. Cover; chill in refrigerator overnight. Cut into thin slices to serve. Yield: 30 servings.

The wigwam smokehouses of S. Wallace Edwards and Sons, Inc., Surry, Virginia.

MARYLAND STUFFED HAM

1 (12-pound) country ham
3 pounds kale, cleaned
2 pounds watercress, cleaned
2 pounds cabbage, cleaned
7 to 8 stalks celery, chopped
1 hot red pepper, chopped
4 cups water
2 tablespoons salt
1 tablespoon pepper
1 tablespoon red pepper
1 tablespoon mustard seed
1 tablespoon celery seed
Cheesecloth

Wash ham, scrubbing thoroughly with a stiff brush. Place ham in a large stockpot; cover with water, and bring to a boil. Boil 20 minutes. Remove ham, and set aside to cool. Discard cooking liquid.

Cut greens into 1½-inch pieces, and place in a large stockpot; add celery and red pepper. Add water; cook over medium heat until greens are limp. Drain well; add remaining ingredients except cheesecloth, and mix well.

Cut 8 lengthwise slits in ham from top of ham to bottom. Stuff each slit with greens mixture. Wrap ham in cheesecloth; secure ends. Place ham in stockpot, fat side up; cover with remaining greens. Add water to cover; bring to a boil. Reduce heat; cover and simmer about 4 hours, or 20 minutes per pound.

Remove stockpot from heat; set aside. Allow ham to cool 2 hours in cooking liquid. Remove ham, and discard greens and cooking liquid. Allow ham to cool to room temperature. Refrigerate overnight. Remove cheesecloth.

Transfer ham to a serving platter. Cut into thin slices to serve. Yield: 24 servings.

S. Wallace Edwards, Jr.

MISSISSIPPI STUFFED HAM

1 (12- to 13-pound) country ham
1 cup vinegar
1 cup sugar
1 onion, peeled and sliced
3 whole cloves
¼ cup whole peppercorns
1 teaspoon red pepper flakes
Stuffing (recipe follows)
¼ cup firmly packed brown sugar
½ cup vinegar

Scrub ham thoroughly with a stiff brush; rinse well. Place ham in a very large container; cover with water. Soak overnight. Drain ham.

Cover ham with cold water; add 1 cup vinegar, sugar, onion, cloves, peppercorns, and red pepper flakes. Cover and bring to a boil. Reduce heat, and cook 4 hours.

Allow ham to cool slightly in cooking liquid. Remove from cooking liquid; drain. Discard cooking liquid. Remove bone and skin from ham; fill cavity with stuffing, and close with skewers.

Place ham, skewered side down, in a shallow roasting pan; sprinkle brown sugar over ham. Pour ½ cup vinegar in bottom of pan. Bake at 325° for 1 hour or until browned. Cool completely.

Transfer ham to a serving platter. Cut into thin slices to serve. Yield: 24 servings.

Stuffing:

2 eggs, beaten
1 onion, finely chopped
1 cup fine dry breadcrumbs
2 tablespoons firmly packed brown sugar
2 tablespoons vinegar
1 tablespoon dry mustard
1 tablespoon celery seeds
1 tablespoon pepper
Red pepper to taste

Combine all ingredients in a small mixing bowl; mix well. Follow directions for stuffing ham in specified recipe. Yield: about 1½ cups.

Pecan-Stuffed Ham, cooked with herbs, spices, and wine.

PECAN-STUFFED HAM

1 (12- to 14-pound) country ham
4 cups pecan halves
1¼ cups fine dry breadcrumbs, divided
2 teaspoons dried whole thyme, divided
2 teaspoons rubbed sage, divided
2 teaspoons ground cloves, divided
2 bay leaves, crushed
¾ cup Madeira wine
1 large onion, chopped
Cheesecloth
¼ cup firmly packed brown sugar

Place ham in a very large container; cover with cold water, and soak overnight. Remove ham from water, and drain. Scrub ham thoroughly with a stiff brush, and rinse well with cold water. Remove bone and ½ pound meat from ham.

Grind pecans and ½ pound ham together using coarse blade of a meat grinder. Stir in 1 cup breadcrumbs, 1 teaspoon thyme, 1 teaspoon sage, 1 teaspoon cloves, bay leaves, and wine. Stuff cavity with pecan mixture. Secure opening with skewers, and tie with string.

Place onion, remaining thyme, sage, and cloves on fat side of ham. Tie ham securely in cheesecloth. Place in a large stockpot; cover with cold water. Bring to a boil. Reduce heat; cover and simmer 3 hours. Allow ham to cool in cooking liquid. Remove ham from cooking liquid, and drain; discard cooking liquid. Remove cheesecloth and skewers. Cut skin and fat from ham; discard.

Place ham, fat side up, in a shallow roasting pan. Top with brown sugar and remaining ¼ cup breadcrumbs. Bake ham, uncovered, at 350° for 30 minutes or until browned. Transfer to a serving platter. Cut into thin slices to serve. Yield: 20 to 25 servings.

BAKED COUNTRY HAM

- 1 (8-pound) country ham, rump portion
- 1 tablespoon whole allspice
- 4 cups firmly packed brown sugar
- 1 cup apple juice

Place ham in a large container; cover with cold water, and soak overnight. Remove ham from water, and drain. Scrub ham thoroughly with a stiff brush, and rinse well with cold water.

Replace ham in container, and cover with fresh cold water. Bring to a boil; reduce heat, and simmer about 2 hours, allowing 15 minutes per pound. Cool. Carefully remove ham from water; remove skin.

Place ham, fat side up, on a cutting board; score fat in a diamond pattern, and stud with allspice. Place ham, fat side up, in a shallow roasting pan. Combine brown sugar and apple juice; mix well. Spoon mixture into bottom of pan around ham. Bake at 350° for 30 minutes, basting occasionally. Transfer to a serving platter; cool completely. Cut into thin slices. Yield: 16 servings.

COUNTRY HAM COOKED IN A BLANKET

- 1 (14- to 15-pound) country ham
- 8 cups all-purpose flour
- 2 cups firmly packed brown sugar
- 1 tablespoon dry mustard
- 1 tablespoon ground nutmeg
- 1 tablespoon ground cinnamon
- 1 tablespoon ground cloves
- 1 tablespoon pepper
- 1 cup water
- 1 cup vinegar
- Topping (recipe follows)
- 1 cup burgundy or other red wine

Place ham in a very large container; cover with cold water, and soak overnight. Remove ham from water, and drain. Scrub ham thoroughly with a stiff brush, and rinse well with cold water. Remove top layer of fat from ham.

Combine flour, brown sugar, mustard, nutmeg, cinnamon, cloves, and pepper in a large mixing bowl; stir well. Add water and vinegar; stir until dry ingredients are moistened.

Turn dough out onto a lightly floured surface; knead 10 to 12 times. Roll dough to ½-inch thickness. Place ham, fat side up, in a lightly greased shallow roasting pan. Place pastry over entire exposed surface of ham.

Bake at 325° for 4 hours. Remove from oven. Remove and discard pastry. Score fat in a diamond pattern. Sprinkle surface of ham with topping. Pour wine into bottom of pan. Bake at 325° for 30 minutes or until browned. Transfer to a serving platter; cool completely. Cut into thin slices to serve. Yield: about 24 servings.

Topping:

- ¼ cup firmly packed brown sugar
- 1 teaspoon dry mustard
- 1 teaspoon ground nutmeg
- 1 teaspoon ground cinnamon
- 1 teaspoon ground cloves

Combine all ingredients; stir well. Yield: about ⅓ cup.

BAKED WHOLE HAM

- 1 (19- to 20-pound) fully cooked ham
- 1 teaspoon pepper
- ½ teaspoon red pepper
- ½ teaspoon garlic salt
- 1 cup firmly packed brown sugar
- ½ cup apple juice
- ½ teaspoon ground cloves

Remove tough outer skin from ham; rinse ham with water. Place ham, fat side up, in a greased shallow roasting pan.

Combine pepper and garlic salt; mix well. Rub surface of ham with pepper mixture.

Combine sugar, apple juice, and cloves; mix well. Set aside.

Bake ham, uncovered, at 300° for 4 hours and 45 minutes; baste every 30 minutes with sugar mixture. Let stand 15 minutes before carving. Yield: 35 to 40 servings.

Baked Whole Ham, the stellar attraction at this picnic, will make sandwiches enough for dozens of hungry people.

The Virginia Blackfords' 1852 recipe for ham sandwiches.

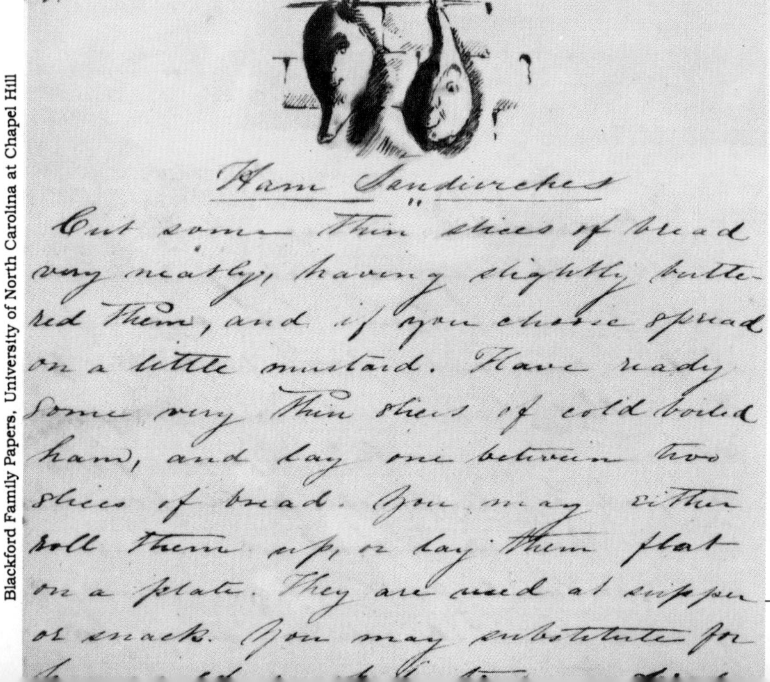

14.

Ham Sandwiches

Cut some thin slices of bread very neatly, having slightly buttered them, and if you choose spread on a little mustard. Have ready some very thin slices of cold boiled ham, and lay one between two slices of bread. You may either roll them up, or lay them flat on a plate. They are used at supper or snack. You may substitute for

Blackford Family Papers, University of North Carolina at Chapel Hill

COLA BAKED HAM WITH APPLESAUCE ASPIC

1 (12-pound) fully cooked ham
1 (67.6-ounce) bottle cola-flavored carbonated beverage
1 (28-ounce) bottle ginger ale
1 cup fine dry breadcrumbs
Applesauce Aspic

Place ham, cola, and ginger ale in a large stockpot. Bring to a boil. Reduce heat; cover and simmer over low heat 4 hours or until tender. Remove ham to a shallow roasting pan; cool.

Carefully remove tough outer layer of skin from ham. Pat fat portion of ham with breadcrumbs. Bake at 325° for 20 minutes or until breadcrumbs are lightly browned. Transfer ham to a serving platter, and let cool 20 minutes before slicing. Garnish with Applesauce Aspic. Yield: 24 servings.

Applesauce Aspic:

1 package unflavored gelatin
¼ cup cold water
1 (16-ounce) can applesauce
½ cup sugar
3 tablespoons lemon juice
¼ teaspoon ground nutmeg
Fresh mint leaves

Soften gelatin in water. Place mixture in top of a double boiler; cook over boiling water, stirring constantly, until gelatin dissolves. Remove from heat; add remaining ingredients, except mint leaves, mixing well. Pour into 5 lightly oiled ⅓-cup molds; chill until firm. Unmold onto a serving platter. Garnish with mint leaves. Yield: 5 (⅓-cup) molds.

Howard W. Odom Papers, Southern Historical Collection, University of North Carolina at Chapel Hill

CHAMPAGNE BAKED HAM

1 (12- to 14-pound) fully cooked ham
1 quart champagne
1 quart water
2 cups sorghum
14 to 16 whole cloves
1 tablespoon prepared mustard
1½ cups firmly packed dark brown sugar
Jelly Sauce

Place ham in a large roasting pan. Pour champagne, water, and sorghum over ham. Cover and bake at 350° for 3 hours and 15 minutes, turning ham in pan every hour to moisten.

Place ham, fat side up, on a cutting board. Trim outer layer of skin. Score fat in a diamond pattern; stud with cloves. Brush mustard over fat; coat with sugar. Broil until sugar melts and forms a glaze.

Transfer ham to a serving platter. Cut into slices, and serve hot with Jelly Sauce. Yield: 20 to 24 servings.

Jelly Sauce:

1 cup grape jelly
2 teaspoons prepared mustard

Combine jelly and mustard in a saucepan; bring to a boil. Cook, stirring often, until jelly dissolves. Yield: 1 cup.

Men in a Model A Ford posed for a Farm Security Administration photograph, one from 1939-40 series taken in North Carolina and Virginia.

Crate labels such as this from Buckingham Bartlett Pears are now collectibles.

BAKED PEANUT HAM WITH SHERRY

1 (10- to 10½-pound) fully cooked ham
1½ cups sherry, divided
½ cup honey
1 tablespoon plus 1 teaspoon whole cloves, divided
¼ teaspoon whole allspice
4 bay leaves
1 cup fine dry breadcrumbs
½ cup firmly packed brown sugar

Place ham, 1 cup sherry, honey, 1 teaspoon whole cloves, allspice, bay leaves, and water to cover in a large container. Bring to a boil. Reduce heat; cover and simmer over low heat 3½ hours or until tender. Cool in cooking liquid. Remove ham from cooking liquid, and remove outer layer of skin. Place ham, fat side up, in a shallow roasting pan.

Combine breadcrumbs, brown sugar, and ½ cup sherry; mix well. Pat outside of ham with breadcrumb mixture. Stud with 1 tablespoon whole cloves. Bake at 350° for 20 minutes or until lightly browned. Transfer ham to a serving platter; cool completely. Cut into slices to serve. Yield: 20 servings.

Ground allspice label.

Smithfield ham is produced on land once owned by one Arthur Smith, for whom the town is named. Virginia's General Assembly moved to protect the reputation of Smithfield's fine ham from imitators when they succinctly "defined" the ham in 1926: "Genuine Smithfield Hams are those cut from the carcasses of peanut-fed hogs raised in the peanut belt of the State of Virginia or the State of North Carolina, and which are cured, treated, smoked and processed in the town of Smithfield, in the State of Virginia."

Virginia State Library

Numbered smokehouses of the Virginia Ham Farms in Clarksville, Virginia, are part of a large operation.

BAKED HAM WITH ORANGE GLAZE

1 (3-pound) canned ham, at room temperature
12 whole cloves
1 tablespoon grated orange rind
½ cup orange juice
2 tablespoons firmly packed dark brown sugar
1 tablespoon prepared mustard
Orange slices (optional)

Place ham on rack in a shallow roasting pan. Bake, uncovered, at 325° for 30 minutes.

Score top of ham in a diamond pattern, and stud with cloves. Combine orange rind, juice, brown sugar, and mustard; spoon half of mixture over ham. Bake 15 minutes.

Spoon remaining orange mixture over ham. Bake an additional 15 minutes, basting frequently with pan drippings. Remove ham to a serving platter. Garnish with orange slices, if desired. Slice and serve hot. Yield: 8 to 10 servings.

BAKED HAM WITH SAUCE

1 (18- to 20-pound) fully cooked ham
15 to 17 whole cloves
1 (10¾-ounce) can beef consommé
1 (16-ounce) jar apple butter
1½ cups sherry
1 cup raisins

Place ham in a large stockpot with water to cover. Bring to a boil. Reduce heat; cover and cook 3 hours. Remove ham from cooking liquid; reserve 1 quart of cooking liquid. Remove outer layer of skin from ham.

Place ham in a large roasting pan. Score fat in a diamond pattern, and stud with cloves. Set ham aside.

Combine reserved 1 quart cooking liquid, beef consommé, apple butter, sherry, and raisins in a large mixing bowl, stirring well. Pour sauce over ham. Bake ham, uncovered, at 350° for 1½ hours or until golden brown, basting frequently with sauce.

Transfer ham to a serving platter; cool slightly. Cut ham into slices, and serve with remaining sauce. Yield: 36 to 40 servings.

SNOW-FROSTED HAM

1 (8- to 10-pound) boneless fully cooked ham
2 (8-ounce) packages cream cheese, softened
1 (8-ounce) carton commercial sour cream
2 tablespoons prepared horseradish, drained
2 teaspoons celery salt
½ teaspoon pepper
½ cup whole maraschino cherries
1 (8-ounce) jar sweet gherkin pickles

Place ham in shallow baking pan, fat side up. Bake, uncovered, at 325° for 2 hours. Set aside, and let cool completely.

Combine cream cheese, sour cream, horseradish, celery salt, and pepper in a large mixing bowl, beating until smooth and creamy. Spread cream cheese frosting on top and sides of cooled ham.

Drain cherries and pickles on paper towels. Cut cherries in half; cut pickles into thin slices. Alternate cherry halves and pickle slices to form a circle, resembling a wreath, on frosted ham. Refrigerate ham at least 1 hour before slicing. Yield: 24 servings.

Snow-Frosted Ham glamorizes a holiday table.

A SLICE OF HAM

BAKED HAM SLICE

½ cup firmly packed brown sugar, divided
1 cup boiling water
3 tablespoons vinegar
1 (5- to 5½-pound) center-cut, fully cooked ham slice, about 3 inches thick
1 teaspoon ground cinnamon
¼ teaspoon ground cloves

Combine ¼ cup brown sugar, water, and vinegar, stirring well. Place ham slice in a greased roasting pan; pour brown sugar mixture over top. Bake, uncovered, at 350° for 1 hour, basting frequently.

Combine remaining brown sugar, cinnamon, and cloves. Sprinkle cinnamon mixture evenly over ham slice. Bake, uncovered, 1 additional hour, basting frequently with pan drippings. Let ham stand 10 minutes before slicing. Yield: 10 to 12 servings.

FRIED HAM WITH MILK GRAVY

2 (¼-inch-thick) center-cut, fully cooked ham slices, about 1½ pounds
½ cup all-purpose flour
1 cup vegetable oil
1 cup milk
¼ teaspoon salt
⅛ teaspoon pepper

Rinse ham slices in warm water; dredge in flour, reserving 2 tablespoons for gravy. Fry ham slices in hot oil in a large skillet over medium heat 4 minutes on each side or until golden brown. Drain well; reserve 2 tablespoons oil in skillet.

Add reserved flour to skillet; cook over medium heat, stirring constantly, 2 to 3 minutes or until flour is lightly browned. Gradually add milk; cook until thickened and bubbly. Stir in salt and pepper. Serve ham with gravy. Yield: 4 servings.

Southerners display their home-canning and ham-curing.

Library of Congress

According to Marion Harland, "Sir Grunter would be a more cleanly creature if he were allowed more extensive water privileges. If it were possible, and in the country this may sometimes be done, to build his pen on the bank of a running stream, he would speedily redeem his character from the stain cast upon it by the popular verdict, and the superior quality of the meat repay the thoughtful kindness of his owner."

HAM IN MUSTARD SAUCE

1 (¾-inch-thick) center-cut, fully cooked ham slice, about 1 pound, quartered
½ cup whipping cream
2 tablespoons prepared mustard
2 tablespoons tomato paste
¾ cup beef broth
2 tablespoons finely chopped onion
1 tablespoon Burgundy or other dry red wine
1 tablespoon chopped fresh parsley
Hot cooked rice

Brown ham pieces in a large skillet. Remove to a warm platter. Set aside and keep warm.

Combine whipping cream, mustard, and tomato paste in a small bowl; stir well, and set aside. Combine beef broth, onion, and wine in skillet. Bring to a boil. Add whipping cream mixture to broth mixture. Cook over low heat 1 minute, stirring constantly. Stir in parsley. Add ham quarters to sauce mixture; cook over low heat 5 minutes or until sauce is slightly thickened. Serve ham and sauce over rice. Yield: 4 servings.

Baked Ham Slice with colorful vegetables.

Memphis Room, Memphis/Shelby County Public Library and Information Center

Horse-drawn wagon holds promotional display of country hams in front of Seessel's Market, Memphis, Tennessee, c.1910.

BAKED HAM STEAK WITH SAUCE

1 (3- to 3½-pound) center-cut, fully cooked ham slice, about 1½ inches thick
1 cup water
½ cup vinegar
½ cup firmly packed brown sugar
1 tablespoon dry mustard
2 tablespoons all-purpose flour

Place ham slice in a 12- x 8- x 2-inch baking dish. Bake, uncovered, at 350° for 30 minutes.

Combine water, vinegar, sugar, and mustard; pour over ham. Bake, uncovered, an additional 30 minutes. Remove ham to a warm serving dish, reserving ham drippings.

Combine ham drippings and flour in a saucepan. Cook over medium heat, stirring constantly, until thickened. Serve sauce over warm ham. Yield: 8 servings.

CRANBERRY-GLAZED HAM SLICE

3 cups fresh cranberries
1½ cups honey
2 (¾-inch-thick) center-cut, fully cooked ham slices, about 3 pounds
1 tablespoon whole cloves

Combine cranberries and honey; stir well. Place 1 ham slice in a 2½-quart shallow baking dish. Spoon half of cranberry mixture over ham slice; place remaining ham slice over cranberry mixture and top with remaining cranberry mixture. Sprinkle with cloves. Bake, uncovered, at 350° for 1 hour; baste frequently with pan juices. Yield: 8 servings.

BAKED HAM WITH PICKLED PEACHES

1 (22-ounce) jar pickled peaches, undrained
1 (2- to 2½-pound) center-cut, fully cooked ham slice, about 1 inch thick
¼ cup firmly packed brown sugar
6 whole cloves

Drain peaches, reserving 1 cup liquid. Set aside.

Place ham slice in a 12- x 8- x 2-inch baking dish. Pour peach liquid over ham; sprinkle with sugar. Insert cloves in ham. Bake, uncovered, at 300° for 45 minutes. Place reserved peaches around ham; bake 15 minutes or until peaches are heated. Serve peaches with ham. Yield: 6 servings.

BAKED HAM WITH SWEET POTATOES

- 4 medium-size sweet potatoes
- 1 (1-inch-thick) center-cut, fully cooked ham slice, about 1½ pounds
- 1 (8-ounce) can pineapple slices, undrained
- ¼ cup dark corn syrup
- 2 tablespoons butter or margarine
- ½ teaspoon ground nutmeg

Place sweet potatoes with water to cover in a small Dutch oven. Boil 30 minutes or until potatoes are tender. Cool and remove peel. Set potatoes aside.

Brown both sides of ham in a large skillet over medium heat. Place ham in a shallow roasting pan. Arrange sweet potatoes around ham. Cut pineapple slices in half; arrange around ham, reserving pineapple juice.

Combine pineapple juice and syrup; pour over ham. Dot with butter, and sprinkle with nutmeg. Cover with aluminum foil; bake at 350° for 30 minutes. Uncover; continue baking 30 minutes, basting occasionally with pan juices. Serve ham with potatoes and pineapple. Yield: 4 servings.

Stylish advertisement for John Bower & Co., late nineteenth century.

Courtesy of the New-York Historical Society

HAM STEAK WITH ORANGE-RICE STUFFING

2 cups cooked regular rice
½ cup raisins
3 tablespoons frozen orange juice concentrate, undiluted
1 egg, well beaten
¼ teaspoon ground nutmeg
¼ teaspoon pepper
2 (½-inch-thick) center-cut, fully cooked ham slices, about 2 pounds
2 tablespoons firmly packed brown sugar

Combine rice, raisins, orange juice, egg, nutmeg, and pepper in a large bowl; stir well. Place one ham slice in a 10- x 8- x 2-inch baking dish. Spoon rice stuffing evenly onto ham slice, and top with second ham slice; sprinkle with brown sugar. Bake, uncovered, at 350° for 35 to 40 minutes. Slice into equal portions. Yield: 6 servings.

HAM-ASPARAGUS ROLLS

¼ cup butter or margarine
2 tablespoons all-purpose flour
1 cup milk
½ cup whipping cream
2 cups (8 ounces) shredded Swiss cheese, divided
½ teaspoon salt
⅛ teaspoon pepper
8 thin slices center-cut, fully cooked ham (about 1 pound)
24 stalks fresh asparagus, cooked and drained

Melt butter in a heavy saucepan over low heat; add flour, stirring until smooth. Cook 1 minute, stirring constantly. Gradually add milk; cook over medium heat, stirring constantly, until thickened and bubbly. Add whipping cream, ¼ cup cheese, salt, and pepper; stir until cheese melts. Set sauce aside.

Place a ham slice on a flat surface; place 3 asparagus spears in center of ham, and top with 2 tablespoons cheese. Roll up jellyroll fashion; place rolls seam side down in a 13- x 9- x 2-inch baking dish. Repeat procedure with remaining ham and asparagus. Pour sauce over ham rolls; sprinkle with remaining cheese.

Broil 4 to 5 inches from heating element 4 minutes or until browned and bubbly. Serve immediately. Yield: 8 servings.

Ham-Asparagus Rolls in rich Swiss cheese and cream sauce.

HAM AND MUSHROOMS À LA KING

½ pound fresh mushrooms, sliced
½ cup plus 2 tablespoons butter or margarine, divided
¼ cup all-purpose flour
1 cup milk
3 tablespoons port wine
1½ cups (6 ounces) shredded Cheddar cheese, divided
⅛ teaspoon red pepper
½ pound sliced cooked ham, divided
Toast points

Sauté mushrooms in 2 tablespoons butter in a medium skillet until tender; set aside.

Melt remaining butter in a 2-quart saucepan over low heat; add flour, stirring until smooth. Cook 1 minute, stirring constantly. Gradually add milk; cook over medium heat, stirring constantly, until thickened and bubbly. Stir in wine, 1 cup cheese, and pepper. Set aside.

Chop half of ham slices; add chopped ham and sautéed mushrooms to cheese sauce. Line bottom and sides of a lightly greased 1-quart baking dish with remaining ham slices. Pour cheese mixture over ham, and sprinkle with remaining cheese. Bake at 350° for 20 to 25 minutes. Spoon hot over toast points. Yield: 4 servings.

DICED AND GROUND HAM

Valentine Museum, Richmond, Virginia

Packing, Curing & Smoking Establishment.

TRY OUR HAMS!

V. HECHLER, JR.
W. T. HECHLER.

Richmond, Va., May 31st 1877

Mr Mann S. Valentine

Bought of V. HECHLER, Jr. & BRO.,
GENERAL PROVISION DEALERS,

Claims for deduction to be made within 5 days from sale.

Nos. 18 and 20 First Market.

May 1	To Mdze bill rendered			36.32
2	3½ lbs Beef			35
11	2¾ " "			47
28	1 Ham 10½	@	15	157
"	2 " 24	"	15	360 $42.31

In May, 1877, Mr. Valentine was paying only 15¢ a pound for ham and less for beef.

CREAMED HAM

3 tablespoons butter or margarine
3 tablespoons all-purpose flour
1 cup milk
1 teaspoon dry mustard
½ teaspoon hot sauce
¼ teaspoon salt
1½ cups cubed, cooked ham
1 cup cubed sharp Cheddar cheese
2 small tomatoes, peeled, seeded, and chopped
¼ cup chopped green pepper

Melt butter in a small saucepan over low heat; add flour, stirring well. Cook 1 minute, stirring constantly. Gradually add milk; cook over medium heat, stirring constantly, until thickened and bubbly. Add mustard, hot sauce, and salt; stir until smooth. Stir in ham, cheese, tomatoes, and green pepper.

Pour mixture into a lightly greased 1-quart casserole. Bake at 350° for 1 hour. Serve over toast points or hot cooked rice. Yield: 4 servings.

HAM AU GRATIN

¼ cup plus 1 tablespoon butter or margarine, divided
3 tablespoons all-purpose flour
1½ cups milk
¾ teaspoon salt
2 cups chopped, cooked ham
4 hard-cooked eggs, chopped
1 teaspoon dry mustard
½ teaspoon pepper
⅓ cup fine, dry breadcrumbs

Melt 3 tablespoons butter in a heavy saucepan over low heat; add flour, stirring until smooth. Cook 1 minute, stirring constantly. Gradually add milk; cook over medium heat, stirring constantly, until thickened and bubbly. Stir in salt.

Combine white sauce, ham, eggs, mustard, and pepper; spoon mixture into a 1½-quart casserole. Sprinkle with breadcrumbs, and dot with remaining butter. Cover and bake at 400° for 15 minutes. Uncover and bake an additional 15 minutes or until lightly browned. Yield: 4 to 6 servings.

Although dry-cured Smithfield ham is frequently compared with the German Westphalian cured ham, there is a difference in the curing method. Westphalian ham is cured by soaking in a brine solution. A better comparison may be drawn between Smithfield and Italian prosciutto, often a feature on antipasto trays. Prosciutto, since it is dry-cured to be served raw in paper-thin slices, is produced under the closest scrutiny of the Italian government.

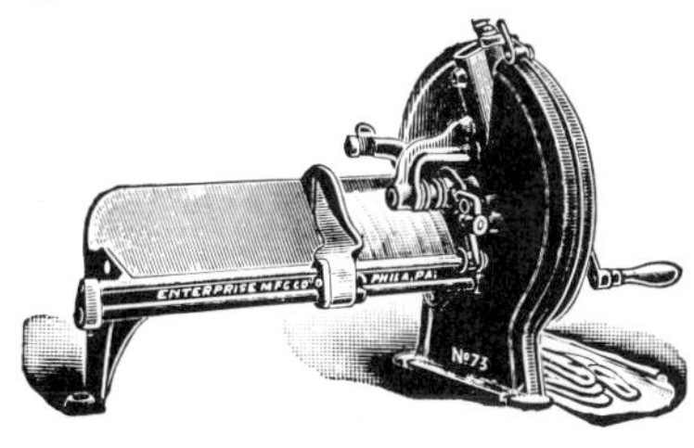

Ham Timbales with Béchamel Sauce. They make an ideal luncheon dish, almost as light as a fluffy soufflé.

BAKED HAM SALAD

2 cups diced, cooked ham
2 cups chopped celery
½ cup chopped almonds
¼ cup sweet pickle relish
1 teaspoon grated onion
Salt to taste
1 cup mayonnaise
½ cup (2 ounces) shredded Cheddar cheese
1 cup crushed potato chips

Combine first 7 ingredients in a large bowl; mix well. Spoon mixture into a 1½-quart casserole; sprinkle with cheese, and top with potato chips. Bake, uncovered, at 400° for 15 minutes or until mixture is bubbly. Serve hot. Yield: 6 servings.

HAM TIMBALES WITH BÉCHAMEL SAUCE

4 eggs
1¼ cups milk
1 teaspoon grated onion
¾ teaspoon salt
⅛ teaspoon pepper
¼ teaspoon paprika
1 cup chopped, cooked ham
¼ cup chopped pimiento
Béchamel Sauce
Additional paprika

Beat eggs in a medium mixing bowl until frothy. Add milk, onion, salt, pepper, and ¼ teaspoon paprika, beating well. Stir in ham and pimiento. Pour mixture into 6 greased ½-cup molds. Place molds in a pan with 1 inch hot water. Cover with greased brown paper. Bake at 350° for 30 minutes or until a knife inserted in center comes out clean.

Cool slightly; loosen edges of timbales with a knife. Invert molds onto a serving plate. Spoon Béchamel Sauce over timbales; sprinkle with additional paprika. Serve hot. Yield: 6 servings.

Béchamel Sauce:

1½ tablespoons butter or margarine
1½ tablespoons all-purpose flour
¾ cup milk
¼ teaspoon salt
Dash of white pepper

Melt butter in a heavy saucepan over low heat; add flour, stirring until smooth. Cook 1 minute, stirring constantly. Gradually add milk; cook over medium heat, stirring constantly, until thickened and bubbly. Stir in salt and pepper. Yield: ¾ cup.

MACARONI AND CHEESE WITH HAM

1¾ cups milk, scalded
1 cup (4 ounces) shredded Cheddar cheese
1 teaspoon grated onion
¼ teaspoon salt
¼ teaspoon paprika
⅛ teaspoon hot sauce
3 eggs, beaten
1½ cups diced, cooked ham
1 cup elbow macaroni, cooked and drained

Combine milk and cheese in a heavy saucepan; cook over low heat, stirring until cheese melts. Remove from heat; stir in onion, salt, paprika, and hot sauce. Gradually stir one-fourth hot mixture into eggs; add to remaining hot mixture, stirring constantly. Stir in diced ham and macaroni. Pour ham mixture into a lightly greased 1½-quart casserole. Bake, uncovered, at 350° for 35 minutes. Yield: 6 servings.

HAM TETRAZZINI

- 1 (7-ounce) package spaghetti
- ¼ cup finely chopped onion
- ½ pound fresh mushrooms, sliced
- ¼ cup butter or margarine
- ½ cup all-purpose flour
- ½ teaspoon salt
- ¼ teaspoon pepper
- ¼ teaspoon garlic salt
- 2 cups milk
- 2 cups half-and-half
- ¾ cup grated Parmesan cheese, divided
- 2 cups diced, cooked ham
- ½ cup fine dry breadcrumbs

Cook spaghetti according to package directions; drain and set aside.

Sauté onion and mushrooms in butter until tender. Add flour, salt, pepper, and garlic salt; stir well. Cook 1 minute, stirring constantly. Gradually add milk and half-and-half; cook over medium heat, stirring constantly, until thickened and bubbly. Set aside.

Toss spaghetti with ½ cup Parmesan cheese. Spoon spaghetti mixture into a lightly greased 2½-quart shallow baking dish. Pour a layer of sauce mixture over spaghetti. Add 1 cup ham; repeat layers, ending with a layer of sauce. Sprinkle remaining Parmesan cheese and breadcrumbs over top. Bake at 350° for 25 minutes. Yield: 6 servings.

Armour's Veribest Food display at the 1917 Texas Women's Fair held at the city auditorium in Houston featured their many quality meat products.

Houston Metropolitan Research Center, Houston Public Library

Overbey/Mobile Public Library Collection, University of South Alabama Photographic Archives

The Southern Gas Company's picnic for employees, held on Mobile Bay, c.1915.

PICNIC PIE

2½ cups all-purpose flour
1¼ teaspoon salt, divided
1 cup shortening
7 to 9 tablespoons cold water
2 cups diced, cooked ham
1 (16-ounce) carton ricotta cheese
1 (12-ounce) carton cottage cheese
⅔ cup grated Parmesan cheese
3 eggs, beaten
1 teaspoon Italian seasoning
¼ teaspoon pepper
1 egg yolk, beaten

Combine flour and ¾ teaspoon salt in a large mixing bowl; cut in shortening with a pastry blender until mixture resembles coarse meal. Sprinkle water evenly over flour mixture; stir with a fork until dry ingredients are moistened. Shape dough into a ball, and wrap in waxed paper. Chill 1 hour.

Combine ham, ricotta cheese, cottage cheese, Parmesan cheese, eggs, Italian seasoning, remaining salt, and pepper in a large mixing bowl; stir until well blended. Set aside.

Roll two-thirds of pastry to ⅛-inch thickness on a lightly floured surface; fit into a 9-inch springform pan. Gently press pastry on the bottom and up the sides of the pan; trim and reserve any overhanging pastry. Spoon cheese mixture into prepared pan, and fold pastry that extends above the filling toward the center of the pan.

Roll remaining chilled pastry to ⅛-inch thickness, and place over filling. Moisten edges, and seal top with bottom pastry. Brush surface of pie with yolk. Using reserved pastry, decorate top crust with small pastry cutouts, and brush again with yolk, if desired.

Bake at 375° for 1 hour. Cool to room temperature; chill. Remove sides from springform pan, and slice to serve. Yield: one 9-inch pie.

Picnic Pie is chilled to make it portable. Satisfyingly hearty with ham and cheese inside, it needs few accompaniments.

HAM SOUFFLÉ

- 2 tablespoons butter or margarine
- 2 tablespoons all-purpose flour
- 2 cups milk
- 3 eggs, separated
- 1 cup fine dry breadcrumbs
- 2½ cups ground smoked ham
- ⅛ teaspoon pepper

Melt butter in a heavy saucepan over low heat; add flour, stirring until smooth. Cook 1 minute, stirring constantly. Gradually add 2 cups milk; cook sauce over medium heat until thickened and bubbly, stirring constantly.

Beat egg yolks until thick and lemon colored. Gradually stir one-fourth hot white sauce into yolks; add to remaining white sauce, stirring constantly. Stir in breadcrumbs, ground ham, and pepper.

Beat egg whites (at room temperature) until stiff but not dry. Gently fold into ham mixture. Spoon into a 1½-quart soufflé dish. Bake at 300° for 1½ hours or until lightly browned. Serve immediately. Yield: 6 servings.

Mary Randolph, a relative of Thomas Jefferson, was an expert ham curer: "When hams have been in salt four weeks, hang them to smoke. If they remain longer on salt they will be hard. Remember to hang the hams and shoulders with hocks down to preserve the juices. Make a good smoke every morning and be careful not to have a blaze. . . . During hot weather, beginning the first of April, it should be occasionally taken down, examined, rubbed with hickory ashes, and hung up again."

HAM STEW

- 1 pound carrots, scraped and sliced
- 3 large onions, peeled and sliced
- 4 stalks celery, sliced
- 1 to 2 tablespoons lemon-pepper marinade
- ½ pound fresh mushrooms, sliced
- 2 cups chopped, cooked country ham
- 1 tablespoon chopped chives
- 1 teaspoon dried whole thyme
- 3 cups milk
- ¼ cup butter or margarine
- 1 cup crushed saltine crackers

Combine first 4 ingredients and water to cover in a stockpot. Bring to a boil. Reduce heat; cover and simmer 30 minutes. Add mushrooms, ham, chives, and thyme; simmer 15 minutes. Stir in milk; cover and simmer (do not boil) 30 minutes. Stir in butter and crackers. Serve hot. Yield: 3 quarts.

STUFFED BELL PEPPERS WITH HAM

6 medium-size green peppers
1 to 1½ pounds ground, cooked ham
2 tablespoons butter or margarine
1 medium onion, chopped
2 medium-size green peppers, chopped
1 clove garlic, minced
3 ripe tomatoes, peeled and finely chopped
2 cups plus 1 tablespoon fine dry breadcrumbs, divided
¼ cup whipping cream
1 tablespoon chopped green onion tops
1 tablespoon chopped fresh parsley
¼ teaspoon salt
¼ teaspoon pepper
⅛ teaspoon red pepper

Cut off tops of 6 green peppers; discard tops and seeds. Cook peppers 4 minutes in boiling salted water to cover; drain and set aside.

Sauté ham in butter in a skillet until browned, stirring occasionally. Add onion, green pepper, and garlic; cook over medium heat until tender. Add tomato; simmer over low heat 1 hour, stirring occasionally. Stir in 2 cups breadcrumbs. Add whipping cream, green onion tops, parsley, salt, and pepper; mix well.

Stuff mixture into green peppers; top with remaining breadcrumbs. Place in a lightly greased, shallow baking dish. Bake at 350° for 30 minutes. Serve hot. Yield: 6 servings.

Given ground, cooked ham plus a few findings, it is appropriate to think of making stuffed eggplant or green peppers.

HAM-STUFFED EGGPLANT

2 medium eggplant
1 medium-size green pepper, chopped
1 medium onion, chopped
2 tablespoons butter or margarine
2 medium tomatoes, peeled and chopped
1 cup diced, cooked ham
½ teaspoon salt
⅛ teaspoon pepper
¼ cup soft breadcrumbs

Wash eggplant; cut a lengthwise slice from top of each eggplant. Remove pulp, leaving a firm shell. Chop pulp, and set aside. Cook eggplant shells in boiling salted water to cover 5 minutes or until tender but firm. Drain; cool slightly.

Sauté green pepper, onion, and reserved eggplant pulp in butter in a large skillet until tender. Stir in tomato, ham, salt, and pepper; cook 1 minute or until thoroughly heated.

Place shells in a 12- x 8- x 2-inch baking dish. Spoon eggplant mixture into shells; top with breadcrumbs. Bake at 350° for 20 minutes or until lightly browned. Yield: 4 servings.

Late 1800s trade card.

The Historic New Orleans Collection, 533 Royal Street

HAM CASSEROLE

1 (14½-ounce) can whole tomatoes, undrained
1 cup regular rice, uncooked
1 cup minced onion
1 cup (4 ounces) shredded Cheddar cheese
1 cup diced celery
1 cup boiling water
¾ pound ground, cooked ham
⅓ cup olive oil
1¼ teaspoons salt
¼ teaspoon pepper

Combine all ingredients in a large mixing bowl, stirring until well blended. Spoon mixture into a lightly greased 2-quart casserole. Cover and bake at 325° for 2 hours or until rice is tender. Yield: 8 servings.

HAM JAMBALAYA

2 slices bacon
2 small onions, finely chopped
1 clove garlic, minced
2 cups canned tomatoes, chopped and undrained
1 tablespoon chopped fresh parsley
2 teaspoons Worcestershire sauce
½ teaspoon salt
¼ teaspoon pepper
1 cup ground, cooked ham
1 cup cooked regular rice

Cook bacon in a medium skillet over low heat until crisp. Remove bacon and reserve for use in another recipe; reserve drippings in skillet.

Sauté onion and garlic in bacon drippings until tender. Add tomatoes, parsley, Worcestershire sauce, salt, and pepper; cook over medium heat 15 minutes, stirring occasionally. Add ham and rice; stir well. Spoon into a lightly greased 1-quart casserole. Bake, uncovered, at 350° for 30 minutes. Yield: 4 servings.

HAM MOUSSE

2 envelopes unflavored gelatin
⅓ cup boiling water
1 cup mayonnaise
1 tablespoon chili sauce
1 teaspoon prepared mustard
⅛ teaspoon red pepper
1 cup whipping cream, whipped
2 cups ground, cooked ham
Fresh parsley sprigs

Dissolve gelatin in boiling water; set aside.

Combine mayonnaise, chili sauce, mustard, and pepper; mix well. Stir in gelatin. Fold in whipped cream and ham. Spoon into an oiled 4-cup mold; chill until firm. Unmold onto a serving platter. Garnish with parsley sprigs. Yield: 10 slices or 14 appetizer servings.

This Prang card, titled The Farm Yard, *was used as a teaching aid in 1874; the scene is not unlike that of a small farm today.*

HAM LOAF

1½ pounds ham
1 pound pork
1 cup vinegar
½ cup firmly packed brown sugar
½ teaspoon dry mustard
½ cup soft breadcrumbs
1 cup milk

Have butcher grind ham and pork together twice.

Combine vinegar, brown sugar, and mustard in a small saucepan; bring to a boil. Boil 1 minute, stirring occasionally. Remove mixture from heat, and set aside.

Soak breadcrumbs in 1 cup milk 5 minutes; add ham mixture, mixing well. Place into a 12-inch cast-iron skillet, and shape into a 12- x 4-inch loaf. Pour vinegar mixture over loaf. Bake loaf, uncovered, at 300° for 1 hour and 20 minutes, basting every 15 minutes with vinegar mixture. Remove loaf to a serving platter. Slice thinly and serve warm or cold. Yield: 10 to 12 servings.

UPSIDE-DOWN HAM LOAF

1 (8¼-ounce) can sliced pineapple, undrained
2 tablespoons butter or margarine, melted
¼ cup firmly packed brown sugar
1 pound ground, cooked ham
½ pound ground lean pork
2 cups soft breadcrumbs
¼ cup finely chopped onion
¾ cup milk
1 teaspoon salt
¼ teaspoon pepper
1 egg, beaten

Drain pineapple, reserving ¼ cup syrup. Pour butter in bottom of an 8½- x 4½- x 3-inch loafpan; arrange pineapple slices over butter, and sprinkle with brown sugar.

Combine remaining ingredients in a medium mixing bowl; mix well. Press mixture over pineapple layer. Bake, uncovered, at 350° for 1½ hours. Drain off excess fat. Invert onto a serving platter. Slice and serve hot. Yield: 6 to 8 servings.

Library of Congress

Library of Congress

Guessing the Pig's Weight *is the title of this sprightly wood engraving by Sol Eytinge. It appeared in* Harper's Weekly *in 1872.*

SAVORY HAM-VEAL RING

1 pound ground, cooked ham
1 pound ground veal
2 cups soft breadcrumbs
¾ cup applesauce
½ cup catsup
½ cup finely chopped onion
2 eggs, beaten
1 teaspoon Worcestershire sauce
½ teaspoon pepper
½ cup apple jelly
2 tablespoons catsup
Cooked Mustard Sauce

Combine first 9 ingredients; mix well. Press mixture into a lightly greased 6½-cup ovenproof ring mold. Bake, uncovered, at 325° for 1½ hours. Invert mold onto a shallow baking pan, and turn meat ring out.

Combine apple jelly and 2 tablespoons catsup in a small saucepan. Cook mixture over medium heat until jelly melts. Pour half of jelly mixture over meat ring, and bake an additional 30 minutes.

Transfer meat ring onto a serving platter. Spoon remaining sauce over ring. Serve with Cooked Mustard Sauce. Yield: 10 to 12 servings.

Cooked Mustard Sauce:

2 tablespoons butter or margarine
1 tablespoon all-purpose flour
1 tablespoon prepared mustard
½ teaspoon salt
¼ teaspoon pepper
¾ cup milk
1 egg yolk, beaten
1 tablespoon lemon juice

Melt butter in top of a double boiler; stir in flour, mustard, salt, and pepper. Combine milk and yolk in a small mixing bowl; gradually stir into flour-mustard mixture. Cook over boiling water 5 minutes or until thickened and smooth. Remove from heat, and stir in lemon juice. Yield: ¾ cup.

Private Collection

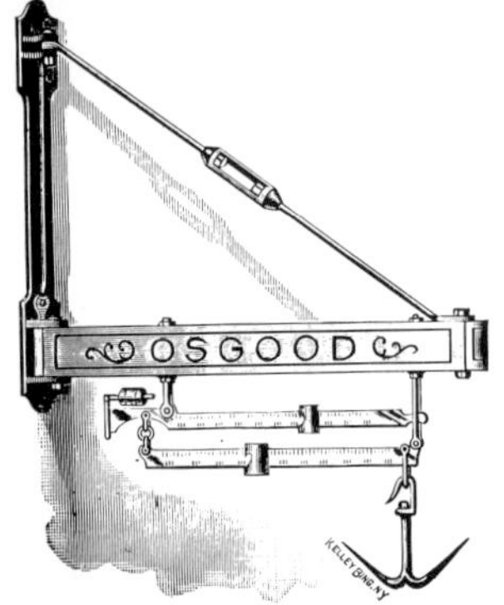

Butcher's Meat Beam

The Farm of Theodor Frick, Porkpacker, at Brook Avenue is an oil on canvas painted by Carl Hambuck, Richmond, Virginia, in 1878. The German-born Frick, a prominent Richmond butcher and sausage maker, purchased the farm in the painting in the late 1860s; his market was located on North Sixth Street. The home remained in the family until 1920 when it was razed to make space for the Ginter Park subdivision. Descendants of the Frick family have inherited many stories about Hambuck, the painter. He is believed to have been trained as a coach- or sign-painter. From atop a house across the street, Hambuck painted the home with family members in the foreground; the artist's self-portrait is visible at bottom left of the painting.

HAM BALLS IN SAUCE

1 medium onion, chopped
2 tablespoons bacon drippings
2 pounds ground, cooked ham
1 cup fine dry breadcrumbs
1 egg, beaten
2 tablespoons prepared mustard
¾ teaspoon salt, divided
½ teaspoon pepper, divided
½ teaspoon marjoram, divided
2 tablespoons butter or margarine
2 tablespoons all-purpose flour
1 (16-ounce) carton commercial sour cream

Sauté onion in bacon drippings until tender. Combine sautéed onion, ham, breadcrumbs, egg, mustard, ½ teaspoon salt, ¼ teaspoon pepper, and ¼ teaspoon marjoram in a large mixing bowl. Mix well, and shape into 2-inch meatballs. Place meatballs in a greased 13- x 9- x 2-inch baking dish; bake at 375° for 30 minutes.

Melt butter in a small saucepan over low heat. Add flour; stir until smooth. Cook 1 minute, stirring constantly. Gradually add sour cream; cook over medium heat, stirring constantly, until thoroughly heated. Stir in remaining salt, pepper, and marjoram.

Spoon sour cream mixture over ham balls; reduce temperature to 300°, and bake an additional 10 minutes. Serve immediately. Yield: 12 servings.

Note: Ham Balls may be made in 1-inch balls for an excellent appetizer.

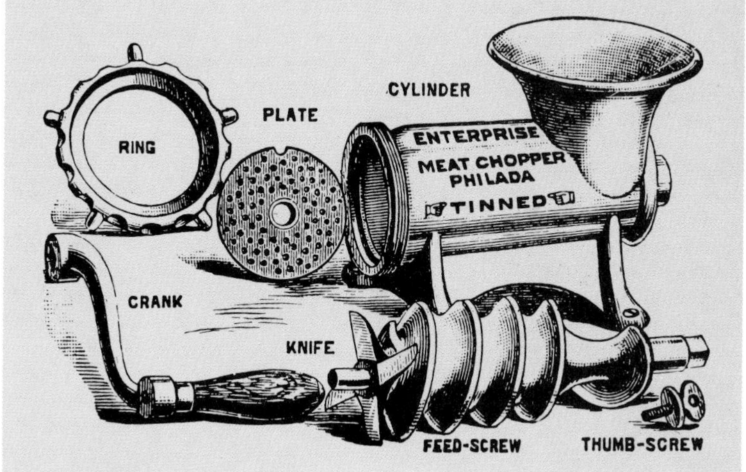

Collection of Bonnie Slotnick

The Enterprise Meat Chopper came with explicit instructions for its assembly and care, 1898.

HAM CROQUETTES

2 tablespoons butter or margarine
¼ cup all-purpose flour
1 cup milk
1 egg, beaten
½ teaspoon paprika
1½ cups ground, cooked ham
1½ cups cooked regular rice
1 egg, beaten
1 tablespoon milk
1 cup fine dry breadcrumbs
3 tablespoons vegetable oil

Melt butter in a heavy saucepan over low heat; add flour, stirring until smooth. Cook 1 minute, stirring constantly. Gradually add 1 cup milk; cook over medium heat, stirring constantly, until thickened and bubbly. Gradually stir 2 tablespoons hot mixture into 1 beaten egg; add to remaining hot mixture, stirring constantly. Stir in paprika. Add ham and rice; mix well. Set aside to cool.

Shape mixture into 12 (2½-inch) croquettes. Combine 1 beaten egg and 1 tablespoon milk; mix well. Dip each croquette into egg mixture, and coat with breadcrumbs. Fry croquettes in hot oil until brown on both sides, turning once. Yield: 1 dozen.

DEVILED HAM

¼ cup butter or margarine
1 tablespoon all-purpose flour
1 cup whipping cream
1½ teaspoons dry mustard
Dash of red pepper
3 cups ground, cooked ham

Melt butter in a heavy saucepan over low heat. Add flour; stir until smooth. Cook 1 minute, stirring constantly. Gradually add whipping cream; cook over medium heat, stirring constantly, until thickened. Stir in mustard and pepper. Add ham; stir well.

Spoon mixture into an oiled 3½-cup mold. Cover and refrigerate at least 4 hours. Unmold onto a serving platter. Serve cold with crackers. Yield: 20 to 24 appetizer servings.

HAM SANDWICH SPREAD

½ pound boiled ham
4 hard-cooked eggs
¼ cup mayonnaise
2 tablespoons sweet pickle relish

Combine all ingredients in container of an electric blender; blend until smooth. Spoon into a serving dish, and refrigerate at least 2 hours. Spread on white or rye bread slices. Yield: 2½ cups.

HAM TURNOVERS

2 tablespoons butter or margarine, divided
1 tablespoon all-purpose flour
½ cup milk
¼ teaspoon salt
⅛ teaspoon pepper
¼ cup chopped onion
2 cups chopped, cooked ham
1 tablespoon chopped fresh parsley
Pinch of dried whole thyme
Pastry (recipe follows)
Melted butter

Melt 1 tablespoon butter in a small saucepan over low heat; add flour, stirring until smooth. Cook 1 minute, stirring constantly. Gradually add milk; cook over medium heat, stirring constantly, until thickened and bubbly. Stir in salt and pepper. Set aside.

Sauté onion in remaining butter in a small saucepan until tender. Combine white sauce, sautéed onion, ham, parsley, and thyme; stir until well blended. Set aside.

Roll pastry to ⅛-inch thickness on a lightly floured surface. Cut into 2-inch circles. Place 1 teaspoon ham mixture on each pastry circle. Moisten edges of pastry; fold in half, making sure edges are even. Press pastry edges firmly together using a fork dipped in flour or with floured fingers.

Place turnovers on lightly greased baking sheets. Brush each turnover with melted butter, and bake at 350° for 45 minutes or until lightly browned. Yield: about 6 dozen appetizer servings.

Pastry:

3 cups all-purpose flour
1½ teaspoons salt
1 cup plus 3 tablespoons shortening
9 to 10 tablespoons cold water

Combine flour and salt in a large mixing bowl; cut in shortening with a pastry blender until mixture resembles coarse meal. Sprinkle water evenly over flour mixture; stir with a fork until dry ingredients are moistened. Shape dough in a ball, and wrap in waxed paper. Chill at least 1 hour or until ready to use. Yield: pastry for 6 dozen 2-inch pies.

SMITHFIELD HAM BISCUITS

2 cups all-purpose flour
1 tablespoon plus 1 teaspoon baking powder
Pinch of salt
2 tablespoons shortening
½ cup ground Smithfield country ham
¾ cup milk

Combine flour, baking powder, and salt. Cut in shortening and ham with a pastry blender until mixture resembles coarse meal. Sprinkle milk evenly over flour mixture, stirring until dry ingredients are moistened.

Turn dough out onto a well-floured surface; knead lightly 8 to 10 times.

Roll dough to ½-inch thickness; cut with a 1¾-inch biscuit cutter. Place biscuits on ungreased baking sheets. Bake at 400° for 10 minutes or until lightly browned. Yield: 2 dozen.

HAM ROLLS

2 cups all-purpose flour
1 tablespoon plus 1 teaspoon baking powder
¼ teaspoon salt
3 tablespoons shortening
1¼ cups milk, divided
1½ cups ground, cooked ham
1 tablespoon minced onion
1 tablespoon minced green pepper
1 tablespoon catsup

Combine flour, baking powder, and salt; stir well. Cut in shortening until mixture resembles coarse meal. Sprinkle ¾ cup milk evenly over flour mixture, stirring until dry ingredients are moistened.

Turn dough out onto a lightly floured surface; knead 10 to 12 times. Roll dough to a 12- x 8-inch rectangle.

Combine ham, ½ cup milk, onion, green pepper, and catsup in a large mixing bowl; stir well. Spread mixture evenly over dough. Roll up jellyroll fashion, beginning at long side; moisten edges with water to seal. Cut roll into twenty-four ¼-inch slices; place slices, cut side down, on greased baking sheets. Bake at 425° for 15 minutes or until rolls are lightly browned. Yield: 2 dozen.

Butcher's sign at Owens Spring Creek Farm.

Photographer: Jim Bathie

Front to rear: Ham Turnovers, Smithfield Ham Biscuits, Ham Rolls.

GLAZES AND SAUCES

COCONUT-PINEAPPLE GLAZE

1 (8-ounce) can crushed pineapple, drained
¼ cup firmly packed brown sugar
1 egg, well beaten
2 tablespoons all-purpose flour
¼ cup flaked coconut
¼ teaspoon ground cinnamon
⅛ teaspoon ground cloves

Combine all ingredients in a small mixing bowl, and mix well. Spoon over baked ham during last 30 minutes of baking time. Glaze may be served with ham. Yield: 1 cup.

CRANBERRY GLAZE

1 (16-ounce) can whole berry cranberry sauce
½ cup light corn syrup

Combine cranberry sauce and syrup in a small mixing bowl; stir well. Spoon over baked ham during last 30 minutes of baking time. Glaze may be served with ham. Yield: 2⅓ cups.

CRANBERRY-RAISIN GLAZE

½ cup firmly packed brown sugar
2 tablespoons cornstarch
Dash of salt
Dash of ground cloves
1½ cups cranberry juice cocktail
½ cup orange juice
½ cup raisins

Combine first 4 ingredients in a medium saucepan. Add remaining ingredients; stir well. Cook over medium heat, stirring frequently, until thickened and bubbly. Remove from heat. Spoon over baked ham during last 30 minutes of baking time. Glaze may be served with baked ham. Yield 2¼ cups.

KEHOE HORSERADISH SAUCE

1 cup whipping cream, whipped
½ cup applesauce
¼ cup prepared horseradish

Combine all ingredients in a medium mixing bowl, stirring well. Serve sauce with baked ham. Yield: 2 cups.

HOT SWEET MUSTARD

¼ cup dry mustard
⅔ cup water, divided
¼ cup sugar
1½ tablespoons cornstarch
½ teaspoon salt
⅓ cup vinegar

Combine mustard and ⅓ cup water in a small mixing bowl; stir until smooth. Set aside.

Combine sugar, cornstarch, and salt in a small saucepan. Gradually add remaining water, stirring until well blended. Add vinegar; stir well. Cook over low heat 5 minutes, stirring constantly. Remove from heat; set aside to cool. Add reserved mustard mixture; stir well. Serve over baked ham or on sandwiches. Yield: 1 cup.

SHERRIED HAM SAUCE

¼ cup catsup
¼ cup sherry
¼ cup butter or margarine
2 tablespoons tarragon wine vinegar
2 tablespoons Worcestershire sauce
1 teaspoon dry mustard

Combine all ingredients in a medium saucepan. Cook over medium heat, stirring constantly, until butter melts. Serve hot with baked ham. Yield: 1 cup.

JEZEBEL SAUCE

1 (5-ounce) jar prepared horseradish
1 (1.12-ounce) can dry mustard
1 (18-ounce) jar apple jelly
1 (18-ounce) jar pineapple preserves
1 tablespoon coarsely ground black pepper

Combine horseradish and mustard in a medium mixing bowl, and stir well. Add remaining ingredients, stirring well. Cover and refrigerate. Serve cold with sliced ham or pork, or on sandwiches. Yield: 4 cups.

SPICED RAISIN SAUCE

2 cups water
1 cup raisins
⅓ cup firmly packed brown sugar
1 tablespoon cornstarch
¼ teaspoon salt
¼ teaspoon dry mustard
¼ teaspoon ground cinnamon
¼ teaspoon ground cloves
1 tablespoon vinegar
1 tablespoon butter or margarine, softened

Combine water and raisins in a medium saucepan. Bring to a boil. Reduce heat; cover and simmer 5 minutes.

Combine next 6 ingredients; stir into raisin mixture. Cook over medium heat, stirring constantly, until thickened. Stir in vinegar and butter. Serve with ham. Yield: 1½ cups.

Succulent baked ham with an array of sauces and glazes. Rear, left to right: Jezebel Sauce, Sherried Ham Sauce, and Kehoe Horseradish Sauce. Front: Hot Sweet Mustard, Cranberry-Raisin and Coconut-Pineapple glazes.

LINKS TO THE PAST

Sausage-making on the East Coast owes as much to the early Germans who came down from Pennsylvania as Texas sausage does to the Germans who entered Texas via Galveston and the Alsatians who settled in and around Bexar County in 1844. These varied ethnic foundations blessed the South with as large a choice of sausage as to be found in any section of the country.

Rudolph's market in Dallas, for example, while selling fresh meat of the highest order, has maintained a sausage factory in the rear of the store since 1895. In addition to the "best klobase west of Pittsburgh," they sell many other irresistible sausages of German, Polish, and Slavic origins.

New Braunfels, Texas, started a Wurstfest in 1961. Exhibits of antique sausage-making equipment, German singing clubs and bands . . . all have contributed to the town's recognition as having one of the most outstanding tourist events of November.

Nowadays, commercially made country sausage is advertised as containing all the best cuts of pork from hams to tenderloin, but sausage began as a thrifty necessity. Fresh and fresh-smoked sausage go back to those early farmers who watched for the first cold snap to get together for hog-butchering. It was a two- or three-day job then, with two or more families helping one another.

After butchering, the farmers trimmed all the excess fat from the various cuts. From this, the leanest trimmings were selected to be ground up for sausage while the fatty trimmings were destined for the lard kettle. In every butchering circle, there was always one person to whom the others deferred for the optimum spicing of the sausage.

In some rural areas, farmers still help one another with hog-butchering and sausage-making. According to tradition, a huge dinner awaits the exhausted crew after their labors. But, thanks to modern equipment, the job is now accomplished in a day. As for the working lard kettle, it is as rare now as the old-time mule-powered sorghum press but is fascinating to anyone whose memories do not include such historic points of reference.

Castroville sausages, ready for a hearty Texas dinner with (clockwise from left): Pickles and onions, German Slaw, Apple-Cherry Crisp dessert, French Bread, and Ranch-Style Potatoes.

CASTROVILLE SAUSAGE DINNER

One reason for the stability of the Castroville, Texas, settlement was that Henri Castro hand-picked the first 700 families, mostly Alsatians, who came there to live. His recruits included farmers, artisans, and educated men who agreed to some firm conditions: Each must have $23 for passage and plenty of clothes, tools, and funds for the first year. On arrival the recruits built homes of limestone, stuccoed and whitewashed, with peaked roofs like the ones they left behind. People and customs endured: This menu is typical of the celebration of the feast of St. Louis which is held in August in Koenig Park. To be entirely authentic, add barbecued beef.

CASTROVILLE SAUSAGE
RANCH-STYLE POTATOES
GERMAN SLAW
DILL PICKLES
SLICED ONIONS
FRENCH BREAD
APPLE-CHERRY CRISP

Serves 8

Early twentieth-century photograph of the St. Louis Society, Castroville, Texas.

CASTROVILLE SAUSAGE

4 pounds ground fresh pork
1 pound ground beef
3 tablespoons plus 1 teaspoon salt
1 tablespoon plus 1 teaspoon ground coriander
1 tablespoon pepper
1 clove garlic, crushed
Dash of ground allspice
Dash of ground cloves
Pork sausage casings (10 to 11 feet)
Cotton string

Combine first 8 ingredients in a large bowl; mix well.

Rinse pork casings thoroughly with warm water; drain. Tie one end of each casing securely with cotton string. Stuff sausage mixture into casings according to basic directions for stuffing sausage (page 98). Twist and tie casings into 12-inch links.

Place sausages, a few at a time, in a large heavy skillet. Add a small amount of water. Cover and cook over low heat 15 minutes. Uncover; drain off liquid, reserving 2 tablespoons in skillet. Cook sausages an additional 10 minutes or until browned, turning to brown completely. Transfer to a serving platter. Yield: 10 (12-inch) links.

RANCH-STYLE POTATOES

8 medium potatoes, cleaned and peeled
1 (12-ounce) package bacon, diced
1 large onion, chopped

Cut potatoes into ¼-inch-thick slices; set aside.

Cook bacon and onion in a large skillet over medium heat until drippings begin to form in bottom of skillet. Add potatoes, and cook, uncovered, 10 minutes or until potatoes are lightly browned. Cover and cook an additional 5 minutes or until potatoes are tender. Yield: 8 servings.

GERMAN SLAW

2 cups boiling water
1 cup vinegar
1 cup vegetable oil
1½ teaspoons sugar
1½ teaspoons salt
1 tablespoon prepared mustard
1 medium cabbage, shredded
1 medium-size green pepper, chopped
Green pepper rings (optional)

Combine water, vinegar, oil, sugar, salt, and mustard in a large mixing bowl. Add cabbage and chopped green pepper, stirring until well blended. Cover and refrigerate overnight.

Drain slaw; spoon into a chilled serving bowl. Garnish with green pepper rings, if desired. Yield: 8 servings.

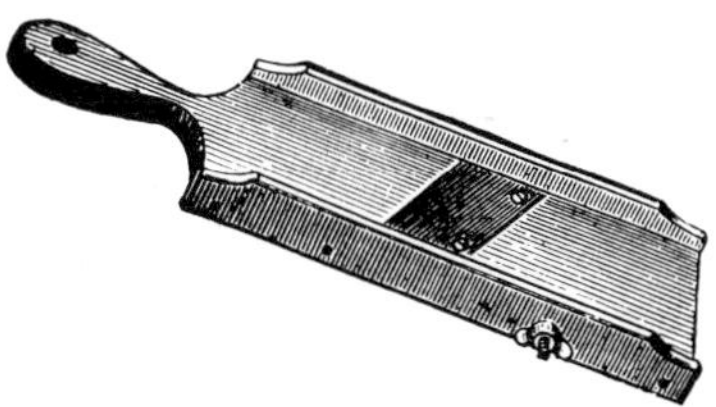

FRENCH BREAD

2 packages dry yeast
2½ cups warm water (105° to 115°)
1 tablespoon butter or margarine
1 tablespoon salt
7 cups all-purpose flour, divided
Yellow cornmeal
1 egg white, well beaten
1 teaspoon salt

Dissolve yeast in warm water in a large mixing bowl; stir well. Add butter and 1 tablespoon salt, stirring until butter melts. Cover and let stand 5 minutes. Stir in 6½ cups flour to form a stiff dough.

Turn dough out onto a surface sprinkled with remaining flour; knead 8 minutes or until dough is smooth and elastic. Place dough in a greased bowl, turning to grease top. Cover and let rise in a warm place (85°), free from drafts, 1½ hours or until doubled in bulk. Punch dough down, and turn out onto a lightly floured surface. Cover and let rest 15 minutes.

Divide dough into thirds; roll each portion into a 13- x 7-inch rectangle. Roll up each rectangle jellyroll fashion, starting at long end. Pinch seams and ends together to seal. Sprinkle 3 heavily-greased baguette pans or baking sheets with cornmeal. Place loaves, seam side down, in baguette pans or on baking sheets.

Cut 3 or 4 diagonal slashes, ¾-inch deep, in top of each loaf. Cover; repeat rising procedure 40 minutes or until doubled in bulk. Combine egg white and 1 teaspoon salt; mix well. Brush on loaves.

Bake at 425° for 30 minutes or until loaves sound hollow when tapped. Remove bread from pans or baking sheets immediately; cool on wire racks. Yield: 3 loaves.

APPLE-CHERRY CRISP

4 large cooking apples, peeled, cored, and sliced
2 (16-ounce) cans tart red pitted cherries, drained
1 teaspoon grated lemon rind
½ cup lemon juice
½ teaspoon ground cinnamon
1 cup all-purpose flour
1 cup sugar
Pinch of salt
½ cup butter, softened
Vanilla ice cream (optional)

Combine apples, cherries, lemon rind, juice, and cinnamon; toss well. Spoon mixture into a lightly greased 13- x 9- x 2-inch baking dish.

Combine flour, sugar, and salt in a large mixing bowl; cut in butter with a pastry blender until mixture resembles coarse meal. Sprinkle topping over fruit mixture. Bake, uncovered, at 350° for 55 minutes or until apples are tender and topping is golden brown. Serve warm with ice cream, if desired. Yield: 8 servings.

FRESH PORK SAUSAGE HOW-TO

FRESH PORK SAUSAGE

3 pounds untrimmed, boneless pork, cubed
1 pound pork fat, cubed
1½ tablespoons salt
1 tablespoon red pepper flakes
1½ teaspoons rubbed sage
¾ teaspoon red pepper
½ teaspoon pepper
Pork sausage casings (5 to 6 feet)

Grind together pork and fat into a large mixing bowl using coarse blade of meat grinder. Add spices; mix well. Grind sausage mixture through meat grinder a second time. Cover and refrigerate overnight to blend seasonings.

Sausage mixture may be stuffed into pork casings and shaped into links, stuffed into muslin casings and sliced into patties, or shaped by hand into individual patties.

To prepare casings for stuffing, cut into desired lengths 30 to 36 inches long, with scissors. Rinse thoroughly with cold running water, allowing the water to run through the casing until salt is removed. Drain well. Tie one end of each casing with cotton string.

To stuff sausage mixture into pork or muslin casings choose one of the following methods, then follow the procedure as identified under the appropriate picture.

To stuff link sausages with an electric meat grinder, follow step 3.

To stuff link sausages with pastry bag, follow step 4.

To stuff muslin casings for sausage patties, follow step 5.

Fresh sausage may be poached in links and broiled, pan-fried, or smoked. Fresh sausage patties may be pan-fried.

To poach, place sausage links in a large skillet. Add ½ cup water per ½ pound sausage. Bring to a boil. Reduce heat; cover and simmer 20 minutes. Remove from heat, and drain well. Pan-fry, broil, or smoke.

To pan-fry, place poached links or patties in a large skillet. Cook over medium heat until browned on all sides, turning to brown evenly. Drain well.

To broil, brush poached links with melted butter. Place on rack in a broiler pan 5 to 6 inches from heating element. Broil 8 to 10 minutes, turning to brown evenly.

Yield: 4 pounds bulk pork sausage or 8 (½-pound) links.

Note: Pork casings may be purchased from the butcher. Store casings in refrigerator, packed in damp salt.

Step 1 — Grind together pork and fat into a large mixing bowl using coarse blade of manual or electric meat grinder.

Step 4 — To stuff link sausages with pastry bag, insert a large, wide-mouth tip into a large pastry bag. Fill bag with sausage mixture. Slip open end of casing over tip of bag. Press sausage mixture into casing using hand to force mixture evenly into casings. Twist into desired links, and tie with string.

Step 2 — Add spices; mix well. Grind sausage mixture through meat grinder a second time. Cover and refrigerate overnight to blend seasonings.

Step 3 — To stuff link sausages with a meat grinder, attach stuffing tube to electric meat grinder. Slip entire length of prepared casing over end of stuffing tube. Turn on machine; press sausage mixture into casing. Do not overstuff casing. Twist filled casings into desired links 4 to 5 inches long; tie between links with cotton string.

Step 5 — To stuff muslin casings, drop small portions of sausage mixture into casing. Press sausage mixture firmly into casing with hands to remove air pockets. Continue filling and pressing sausage mixture into casing until 2½ inches of casing remains. Twist top of casing tightly; tie with cotton string.

Step 6 — Fresh sausage links are first poached and then broiled, pan-fried, or smoked. Sausage patties are pan-fried.

HOMEMADE SAUSAGE

KENTUCKY PORK SAUSAGE

4 pounds pork tenderloin, cubed
2 pounds pork fat
2 tablespoons salt
2 tablespoons rubbed sage
1 tablespoon pepper
2 teaspoons ground coriander
2 teaspoons ground nutmeg
¾ teaspoon red pepper

Grind together tenderloin and fat into a large mixing bowl using coarse blade of meat grinder. Add remaining ingredients; mix well. Grind sausage mixture a second time.

Divide mixture into three 2-pound portions. Shape each portion into a roll, 2 inches in diameter; wrap in waxed paper. Refrigerate overnight.

Slice sausage rolls into ½-inch-thick patties. Cook in a skillet over medium heat until browned, turning once. Drain. Yield: 3 (2-pound) rolls or 6 dozen (½-inch) patties.

Note: Sausage rolls may be frozen. Thaw in refrigerator before slicing into patties.

COUNTRY SAUSAGE

½ pound untrimmed boneless pork, cubed
½ pound boneless veal, cubed
½ pound pork fat
1 cup soft breadcrumbs
2 teaspoons grated lemon rind
2 teaspoons salt
½ teaspoon pepper
¼ teaspoon ground marjoram
¼ teaspoon rubbed sage
¼ teaspoon ground thyme
⅛ teaspoon ground summer savory

Grind together pork, veal, and fat into a mixing bowl using fine blade of meat grinder. Repeat procedure. Add remaining ingredients, mixing well.

Shape sausage mixture into a roll, 1½ inches in diameter. Wrap roll in waxed paper, and refrigerate overnight to blend seasonings.

Slice sausage roll into ½-inch-thick patties. Cook patties in skillet over medium heat until browned on both sides, turning once. Drain; serve immediately. Yield: 1 (1½-pound) roll or 2½ dozen (½-inch) patties.

CHORIZO

4½ pounds boneless pork roast, cubed
1 large onion, finely chopped
3 tablespoons red wine vinegar
1 tablespoon plus 2 teaspoons red pepper
1 tablespoon plus 2 teaspoons coarsely ground black pepper
2 tablespoons salt
2 tablespoons brandy
1 tablespoon red pepper flakes
1 tablespoon fennel seeds
5 large cloves garlic, minced
1 teaspoon ground cumin
Pork sausage casings (6 to 9 feet)
½ cup water, divided

Grind pork into a large mixing bowl using coarse blade of meat grinder. Add next 10 ingredients; mix well. Grind mixture through meat grinder a second time. Cover; refrigerate 4 hours to blend flavors.

Rinse pork casings thoroughly with warm water; drain. Tie one end of each casing securely with cotton string. Stuff sausage mixture into casings according to basic directions for stuffing sausage. Twist and tie casings into 8-inch links. (Sausage links may be cooked immediately, refrigerated 3 to 4 days, or frozen for later use.)

Place half of links in a large skillet; pierce each link with a needle 3 to 4 times. Add ¼ cup water. Cover; simmer 10 minutes. Uncover and cook over low heat, turning sausage frequently, until water evaporates. Repeat procedure with remaining sausage links and water. Slice and serve warm or use in other sausage recipes. Yield: 9 (½-pound) links.

1800s weathervane hog. Rooster and cow vanes replaced them in popularity.

Abby Aldrich Rockefeller Folk Art Center, Williamsburg, Virginia

Assorted sausages from top: Chorizo, Bratwurst, Kielbasa, and Country Sausage.

KLOBASE

8 pounds boneless pork, cubed
2 pounds ground beef
½ cup water
3½ tablespoons salt
1½ tablespoons pepper
1 teaspoon rubbed sage
1 teaspoon garlic salt
6 cloves garlic, minced
Pork sausage casings (18 to 20 feet)
2 tablespoons shortening

Grind pork into a large mixing bowl using coarse blade of meat grinder. Add ground beef, ½ cup water, salt, pepper, sage, garlic salt, and garlic; mix well.

Rinse pork casings thoroughly with warm water; drain. Tie one end of each casing securely with cotton string. Stuff sausage mixture into casings according to basic directions for stuffing sausage. Twist and tie casings into 8-inch links. Refrigerate 24 hours to blend flavors. (Sausage links may be cooked immediately, refrigerated 3 to 4 days, or frozen for later use.)

Place 4 to 5 sausage links in a large skillet; pierce each link with a needle 3 to 4 times. Add water to skillet to depth of ½-inch. Cover and simmer over low heat 50 minutes or until lightly browned, turning occasionally. Slice and serve warm or use in other sausage recipes. Yield: 40 (¼-pound) links.

KIELBASA

5 pounds ground fresh pork
¾ cup water
8 cloves garlic, minced
2 tablespoons salt
2 teaspoons pepper
¾ teaspoon rubbed sage
½ teaspoon caraway seeds
½ teaspoon red pepper
Pork sausage casings (6 to 7 feet)
Hickory chips soaked in water

Combine first 8 ingredients in a large mixing bowl, mixing well. Set pork mixture aside.

Rinse pork casings thoroughly with warm water; drain. Tie one end of each casing securely with cotton string. Stuff sausage mixture into casings according to basic directions for stuffing sausage. Twist and tie casings into 12-inch links. Set links aside.

Prepare charcoal fire in smoker, and let burn 10 to 15 minutes. Sprinkle wet hickory chips over grey-white coals. Place water pan in smoker, and fill with hot water.

Place lower food rack on appropriate shelf in smoker. Arrange half of sausage links on rack. Place upper food rack on shelf, and arrange remaining sausage links on rack. Cover smoker with lid. Smoke sausage links 6 to 12 hours, refilling water pan with additional water, if needed. Remove sausage links from smoker. Slice and serve immediately or refrigerate for later use. Yield: 6 (¾-pound) sausage links.

A sausage recipe from 1893: "Sausage Meat: Seven pounds of fat and twelve pounds of lean meat. To this quantity, put six table-spoonfuls of sage; six of salt; three of savory; and three of pepper."

50 Years in a Maryland Kitchen

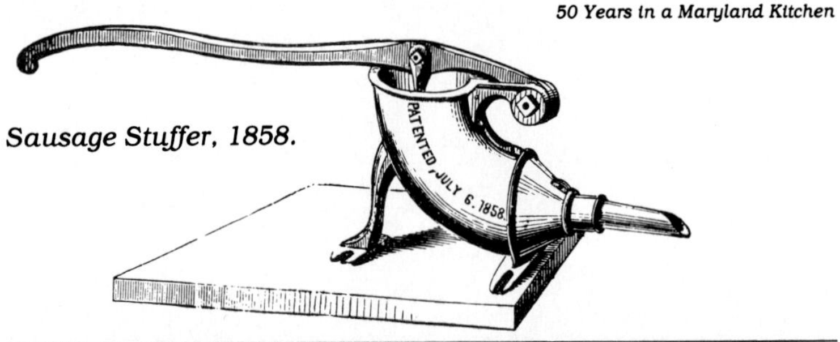

Sausage Stuffer, 1858.

SAUER-BECKMAN BRATWURST

3 pounds boneless beef, cubed
2 pounds boneless pork, cubed
3 tablespoons plus 1 teaspoon pickling salt
1 tablespoon plus 2 teaspoons coarsely ground black pepper
½ teaspoon saltpeter
Pork sausage casings (9 to 10 feet)
Hickory chips soaked in water

Grind together beef and pork into a large mixing bowl using coarse blade of meat grinder. Add pickling salt, pepper, and saltpeter; mix well. Grind sausage mixture through meat grinder a second time.

Rinse pork casings thoroughly with warm water; drain. Tie one end of each casing securely with cotton string. Stuff sausage mixture into casings according to basic directions for stuffing sausage. Twist and tie casings to form 6-inch links. Set links aside.

Prepare charcoal fire in smoker, and let burn 10 to 15 minutes. Sprinkle wet hickory chips over grey-white coals. Place water pan in smoker, and fill with hot water.

Place lower food rack on appropriate shelf in smoker. Arrange half of sausage links on rack. Place upper food rack on shelf, and arrange remaining sausage links on rack. Cover smoker with lid. Smoke 4 to 5 hours, refilling water pan with additional water, if needed. Remove sausage links from smoker, and use immediately in other recipes or freeze until ready to use. Yield: 20 (¼-pound) links.

Lyndon B. Johnson Park

Bill Reaves

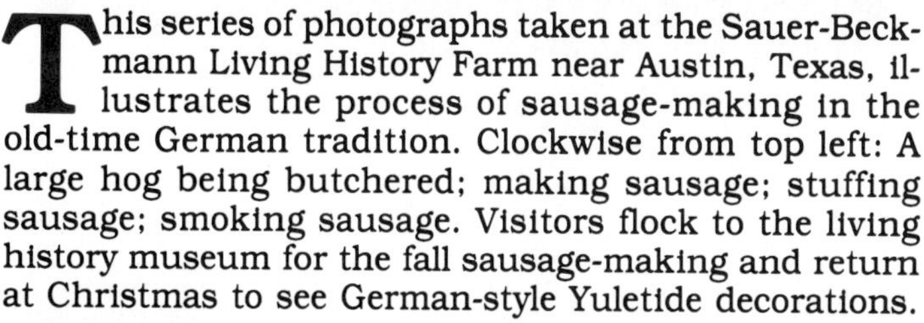

This series of photographs taken at the Sauer-Beckmann Living History Farm near Austin, Texas, illustrates the process of sausage-making in the old-time German tradition. Clockwise from top left: A large hog being butchered; making sausage; stuffing sausage; smoking sausage. Visitors flock to the living history museum for the fall sausage-making and return at Christmas to see German-style Yuletide decorations.

Lyndon B. Johnson Park

Lyndon B. Johnson Park

SAUSAGE MAKES A MEAL

Hog Killing Time, *oil on canvas painted by Harold Osman Kelly.*

TOAD-IN-THE-HOLE

1 cup milk
2 eggs
1 cup all-purpose flour
½ teaspoon salt
1 pound bulk pork sausage
Maple syrup (optional)

Combine milk and eggs in a mixing bowl; mix well. Add flour and salt, beating until smooth. Cover; set aside 1 hour.

Shape sausage into 6 patties, 3½ inches in diameter and about ½-inch thick. Cook patties in skillet over medium heat until done, turning once. Drain sausage patties, reserving 2 tablespoons pan drippings.

Place pan drippings in a 10- x 6- x 2-inch baking dish. Arrange sausage patties in dish. Pour batter over sausage patties. Bake, uncovered, at 450° for 30 minutes or until browned. Serve warm with maple syrup, if desired. Yield: 4 to 6 servings.

Harold Osman Kelly, 1884-1955, left home in Bucyrus, Ohio, at age 16 and worked his way through 30 states as a jack-of-all-trades. His wife, Jessie, whom he married in Arkansas while he was sharecropping, moved with him to the Texas Panhandle. Their ranch was wiped out by the dust storms of the 1930s. Resettled in Blanket, Texas, he turned to painting when in his 50s; his avocation became his career.

SAUSAGE PIE

1 pound bulk pork sausage
1 cup fine dry breadcrumbs
½ cup chopped onion
⅓ cup catsup
¼ cup prepared mustard
2 eggs, beaten
1 tablespoon dried parsley flakes
1 tablespoon Worcestershire sauce
¼ teaspoon garlic salt
1 baked (9-inch) pastry shell
1 cup (4 ounces) shredded Cheddar cheese

Crumble sausage in a medium skillet; cook over medium heat until browned, stirring occasionally. Drain well. Add breadcrumbs, onion, catsup, mustard, eggs, parsley, Worcestershire sauce, and garlic salt, stirring well.

Spread sausage mixture evenly in pastry shell. Bake at 350° for 20 minutes. Sprinkle with cheese, and bake an additional 5 minutes. Cut into wedges, and serve hot or cold. Yield: one 9-inch pie.

Note: Hot or mild sausage would complement this combination of ingredients.

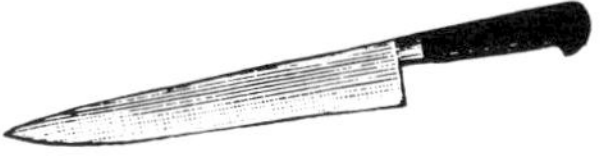

SAUSAGE-CHEESE CASSEROLE

1 pound hot bulk pork sausage
2 medium onions, chopped
1 medium-size green pepper, chopped
1 (14½-ounce) can whole tomatoes, chopped and undrained
1 cup macaroni, uncooked
1 tablespoon sugar
1 (8-ounce) carton commercial sour cream
½ cup grated Parmesan cheese, divided

Combine sausage, onion, and green pepper in a large skillet; cook until sausage is browned, stirring to crumble meat. Drain well. Add tomatoes, macaroni, and sugar, stirring until well blended. Cover and simmer 20 minutes.

Remove from heat; stir in sour cream and ¼ cup cheese. Spoon mixture into a 1½-quart casserole. Sprinkle top with remaining cheese, and serve immediately. Yield: 6 servings.

APPLE-SAUSAGE LOAF

4 medium-size sweet potatoes
1 pound bulk pork sausage
1⅓ cups soft breadcrumbs
⅓ cup evaporated milk
⅓ cup applesauce
¼ teaspoon salt, divided

Cook sweet potatoes in boiling water to cover 35 minutes or until tender. Drain; let cool to touch. Peel and cut into quarters. Set aside.

Combine sausage, breadcrumbs, milk, applesauce, and ⅛ teaspoon salt in a large bowl. Shape meat mixture into a loaf; place in a lightly greased 13- x 9- x 2-inch baking pan. Bake at 350° for 1 hour. Add quartered sweet potatoes, and sprinkle with remaining salt. Bake an additional 20 minutes, basting potatoes frequently with pan drippings.

Remove meat loaf and potatoes to a warm serving platter; discard pan drippings. Slice meat loaf. Serve with sweet potatoes. Yield: 4 servings.

Woman making sausage. Photo by Russell Lee, 1939.

Library of Congress

Dallas Museum of Art, Dallas Art Association Purchase

PURE LARD

Owens Sausage Stew is an easy-to-make, satisfying dish for the family.

OWENS SAUSAGE STEW

- 2 pounds hot bulk pork sausage
- 1 (17-ounce) can green peas, undrained
- 1 (16-ounce) can cut green beans, undrained
- 1 (14½-ounce) can whole tomatoes, undrained
- 1 (12-ounce) can whole kernel corn, undrained
- 3 (8-ounce) cans tomato sauce
- 4 large baking potatoes, peeled and diced
- 2 carrots, scraped and cut into ½-inch slices

Shape sausage into large patties. Cook patties in skillet over medium heat until done, turning once. Drain; break patties into large chunks. Set aside.

Combine remaining ingredients in a large saucepan with water to cover; stir well. Bring to a boil. Reduce heat; simmer, uncovered, 15 minutes. Reduce heat to low; stir in sausage, and simmer an additional 45 minutes or until potatoes are tender. Yield: about 3 quarts.

Mama canned sausage because there was no other way to preserve it for a long period. . . . Roll freshly ground sausage into patties. Put in large skillet and cook until done. Put in sterile jars and seal. Turn jars upside down until cold. The excess grease will go to the top of the jar, sealing in freshness. When ready to eat, remove from jars and heat. What a treat when all the fresh meat is gone!

Heart of Texas Cookbook

SAUSAGE-CHEESE DIP

- 1½ pounds hot bulk pork sausage
- ½ pound ground chuck
- 1 (10¾-ounce) can cream of mushroom soup, undiluted
- 1 (10-ounce) jar tomato sauce with jalapeño peppers
- 1 (4-ounce) can chopped green chiles, undrained
- 1 medium onion, chopped
- 3 cloves garlic, minced
- 2 pounds process cheese spread, cut into 1-inch cubes

Brown sausage and ground chuck in a medium Dutch oven, stirring to crumble; drain off pan drippings. Add mushroom soup, tomato sauce, chiles, onion, and garlic; stir until well blended. Simmer 20 minutes, stirring occasionally.

Add cheese, and cook over low heat, stirring until cheese melts. Serve warm with chips. Yield: 8 cups.

SAUSAGE WITH APPLES

- 4 (½-pound) fresh Country sausage links
- 4 medium-size cooking apples, cored and thinly sliced
- ¼ cup firmly packed brown sugar

Place sausage links on rack in a broiler pan. Place 6 to 7 inches from heating element, and broil for 2 to 3 minutes or until sausage links are lightly browned. Reduce heat to 350°, and bake an additional 10 minutes.

Arrange apple slices around sausage links on broiler rack; sprinkle with brown sugar. Bake 15 minutes or until apples are tender. Yield: 4 servings.

SAUSAGE ROLLS

- 3 (½-pound) fresh Country sausage links
- 2 cups all-purpose flour
- ½ teaspoon baking powder
- ½ teaspoon salt
- ⅓ cup boiling water
- ⅔ cup shortening
- 1 egg, beaten

Pierce sausages several times with a fork. Place sausages in a large Dutch oven with water to cover; bring to a boil. Reduce heat; cover and cook 15 to 20 minutes.

Drain sausages on paper towels. Remove casings from sausages; discard casings. Cut each sausage in half lengthwise, and set aside.

Combine flour, baking powder, and salt in a small mixing bowl. Stir well, and set aside.

Pour boiling water over shortening in a large mixing bowl; beat at high speed of an electric mixer until creamy. Add flour mixture, stirring until well blended. Chill in refrigerator 10 minutes.

Roll pastry to ¼-inch thickness on a lightly floured surface. Cut pastry into six 5-inch squares. Place a sausage half in center of each pastry square. Moisten edges of square; fold pastry in half to form rectangles. Press edges firmly together to seal.

Place on a lightly greased baking sheet, and brush with beaten egg. Bake at 425° for 10 minutes or until lightly browned. Yield: 6 rolls.

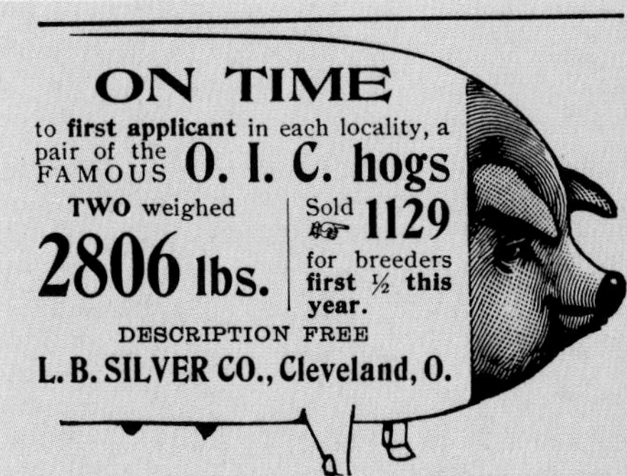

Library of Congress

Threshing machines at work in the rice fields of Lake Charles, Louisiana.

GERMAN SAUSAGE DISH

1 medium cabbage, quartered
1½ teaspoons salt, divided
2 (12-ounce) packages smoked sausage links
2 cups cooked, mashed potatoes
1½ tablespoons butter or margarine
¼ teaspoon pepper

Combine cabbage, 1 teaspoon salt, and water to cover in a medium Dutch oven. Bring to a boil. Reduce heat; cover and simmer 25 minutes. Add sausages; cover and simmer an additional 30 minutes. Remove sausages; set aside, and keep warm. Drain cabbage and chop; set aside.

Combine potatoes, butter, remaining salt, and pepper in a large mixing bowl; beat until well blended. Add chopped cabbage, and stir until well blended. Spoon cabbage mixture onto a warm serving platter. Place sausage links on top of cabbage mixture, and serve immediately. Yield: 4 to 6 servings.

Rice was introduced to the New World by way of South Carolina in 1680, but its ready acclimatization to Southern growing conditions fostered its production throughout the Southern colonies. In Louisiana, rice found a particularly welcome home: The flatlands were ideal for its growth, and the Acadians and Creoles considered it a basic in their cuisine. So basic is this nutritious grain in the area, it is often served three times a day. No wonder Louisianians are said to consume more rice in one year than most Americans consume in five years.

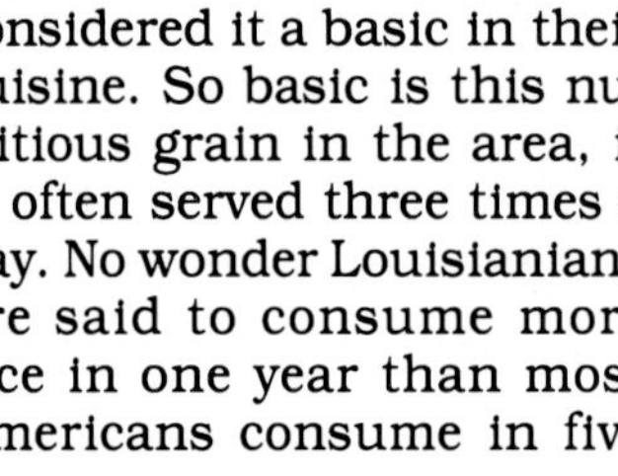

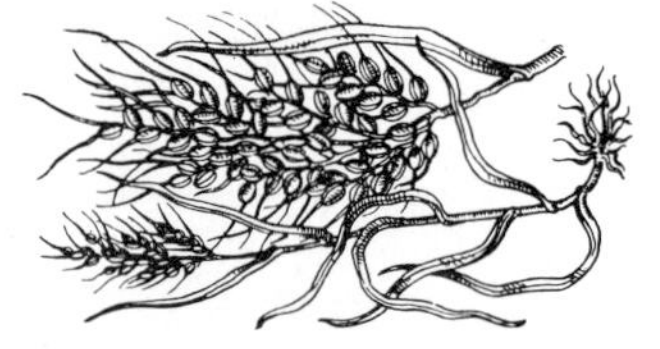

SAUSAGE SAUCE PIQUANT

1 tablespoon all-purpose flour
1 tablespoon vegetable oil
1 (1-pound) package fresh Country sausage links, diced
1 small onion, chopped
1 small green pepper, chopped
1 (14½-ounce) can whole tomatoes, undrained and diced
¼ cup water
Salt and pepper to taste
Hot cooked rice

Combine flour and oil in a large skillet. Cook over medium heat, stirring constantly, until browned. Add sausage, onion, and green pepper; cook until vegetables are tender. Stir in tomatoes and water. Cover and simmer 1 hour, stirring occasionally. Add salt and pepper to taste. Serve over hot cooked rice. Yield: 4 servings.

CHICKEN-SAUSAGE JAMBALAYA

1 tablespoon salt
1½ teaspoons pepper
1½ teaspoons red pepper
1 (6- to 6½-pound) baking hen, cut up
1 cup vegetable oil
1 large onion, chopped
3 cloves garlic, minced
2 pounds smoked sausage links, cut into 1-inch pieces
3 quarts water
¼ cup chopped green onion
2 tablespoons chopped fresh parsley
4 cups regular rice, uncooked

Combine salt and pepper; sprinkle evenly over chicken pieces, coating well.

Heat oil in a large Dutch oven. Add chicken pieces, a few at a time. Brown on all sides; drain on paper towels. Set aside. Reserve oil in Dutch oven.

Add onion and garlic to Dutch oven; sauté until onion is tender. Remove onion and garlic; drain well, and set aside. Add sausage to Dutch oven. Cook over medium heat until browned. Drain on paper towels. Discard pan drippings.

Return chicken pieces, onion, garlic, sausage, and water to Dutch oven. Bring to a boil. Reduce heat; cover and simmer 2½ hours or until chicken is tender. Add green onion, parsley, and rice; stir well. Cover and cook over low heat 45 minutes or until liquid is absorbed. Yield: 6 quarts.

CREOLE JAMBALAYA

1 pound lean pork, cubed
3 medium onions, chopped
1 medium-size green pepper, chopped
2 cloves garlic, minced
2 tablespoons chopped fresh parsley
2 tablespoons butter or margarine
1 cup diced fully cooked ham
1 teaspoon chili powder
½ teaspoon ground cloves
½ teaspoon pepper
⅛ teaspoon red pepper
1 (12-ounce) package smoked sausage links, cut into 1-inch pieces
2 quarts beef broth
1½ cups regular rice, uncooked
Chopped fresh parsley

Sauté pork, onion, green pepper, garlic, and 2 tablespoons parsley in butter in a large Dutch oven until meat is browned and vegetables are tender. Stir in ham, chili powder, cloves, pepper, and sausage. Cook over medium heat 10 minutes, stirring frequently.

Add broth and rice; mix well. Cover and simmer 20 minutes or until rice is tender, stirring occasionally. Garnish with chopped fresh parsley. Serve hot. Yield: 3½ quarts.

Creole Jambalaya, a Southern stew with rice cooked in it, is seldom found outside the region. A great reason to travel.

RED BEANS AND RICE

1 (16-ounce) package dried red kidney beans
1 ham bone
3 quarts water
2 teaspoons garlic salt
Hot sauce to taste
1 teaspoon Worcestershire sauce
1 cup chopped celery
1 cup chopped onion
1½ cloves garlic, minced
3 tablespoons vegetable oil
½ pound ham, cubed
¼ pound hot bulk pork sausage, sliced
½ pound smoked sausage links, sliced
2 bay leaves
Salt and pepper to taste
Hot cooked rice

Sort and wash beans; place in a large Dutch oven with water to cover 2 inches above beans. Cover and let soak overnight. Drain beans well.

Combine beans, ham bone, 3 quarts water, garlic salt, hot sauce, and Worcestershire sauce in Dutch oven. Bring to a boil. Reduce heat; cook, uncovered, 20 minutes.

Sauté celery, onion, and garlic in oil in a large skillet until tender. Add to bean mixture, reserving oil in skillet.

Add ham and sausage to skillet; cook until browned. Add ham and sausage, bay leaves, and salt and pepper to bean mixture; stirring well. Cook, uncovered, over medium heat 2½ hours or until beans are tender, stirring occasionally. Remove bay leaves, and discard. Serve over hot cooked rice. Yield: 10 servings.

When the late Carl Fletcher and his brother, Neil, were offered a booth at the Texas State Fair back in 1938, they began to think of coating hot dogs with a cornmeal batter and serving them impaled on a stick. It took them a few years to perfect a method for keeping the batter on the dog.

The recipe finally clicked in 1943, and that year, the Fletchers, former vaudevillians, grossed about $8,000 at 15¢ for every corny dog. Their enterprise resulted in a family business, now run by Neil's sons, Neil Jr., Bill, and John, worth some half million a year, serving two Dallas locations.

Clint Grant

Strolling the midway, a couple enjoy corny dogs at the Texas State Fair, an institution since 1886.

Make your own Corny Dogs, much like those developed for the Texas State Fair in 1943.

FRANKS IN BARBECUE SAUCE

1 medium onion, chopped
2 tablespoons butter or margarine
1 cup catsup
½ cup vinegar
1 teaspoon salt
1 teaspoon pepper
1 teaspoon sugar
1 teaspoon paprika
1 teaspoon chili powder
1 teaspoon prepared mustard
½ teaspoon hot sauce
½ teaspoon Worcestershire sauce
10 frankfurters

Sauté onion in butter in a large skillet until tender. Add catsup, vinegar, salt, pepper, sugar, paprika, chili powder, mustard, hot sauce, and Worcestershire sauce; stir until well blended. Cover and simmer 20 minutes, stirring frequently.

Slice frankfurters in half lengthwise; drop into boiling water. Remove from heat; cover and let stand 5 minutes. Drain.

Add frankfurters to barbecue sauce, stirring to coat well. Cover and simmer 5 minutes or until frankfurters are thoroughly heated. Serve immediately. Yield: 10 servings.

CORNY DOGS

¾ cup all-purpose flour
¾ cup cornmeal
1 tablespoon plus 1 teaspoon baking powder
2 teaspoons dry mustard
½ teaspoon salt
1 cup milk
2 eggs, beaten
10 frankfurters
10 wooden skewers
Vegetable oil
Prepared mustard (optional)
Catsup (optional)

Combine flour, cornmeal, baking powder, mustard, and salt in a medium mixing bowl; stir well. Combine milk and egg in a small mixing bowl; add to dry ingredients, stirring well. Set aside.

Wipe each frankfurter dry, and insert a wooden skewer into one end. Dip frankfurters in batter; fry in deep hot oil (375° to 400°) for 3 minutes or until browned, turning once. Drain well on paper towels. Repeat with remaining frankfurters. Serve with mustard and catsup, if desired. Yield: 10 servings.

When we put sauerkraut together with cured, ready-to-eat sausages, we are combining two very old preserved foods. Fermented cabbage went with old-time mariners on long voyages; it gave them some vitamins and a hint of freshness in their diet. German and Polish settlers brought sausage-making techniques to this country, as did the French and Mexican-Spanish. Sauerkraut too sour? Temper it by rinsing; apples sweeten it.

KLOBASE WITH SAUERKRAUT

1 pound fully cooked Klobase sausage
1 (16-ounce) can shredded sauerkraut, undrained
¾ cup water
1 teaspoon caraway seeds
½ teaspoon salt
1 small potato, peeled and shredded
1 small onion, chopped
1 tablespoon shortening
1 tablespoon all-purpose flour

Cut sausage into 2-inch pieces. Place sausage with water to cover in a large Dutch oven; bring to a boil. Reduce heat; cover and cook 10 minutes or until thoroughly heated. Remove from water; set aside, and keep warm.

Combine sauerkraut, water, caraway seeds, and salt in a medium Dutch oven. Bring to a boil; reduce heat, and simmer 10 minutes. Stir in potato; simmer 3 minutes.

Sauté onion in hot shortening in a small skillet until tender. Stir in flour; cook 1 minute. Spoon onion mixture into sauerkraut mixture, stirring well. Cook over medium heat, stirring constantly, 3 to 5 minutes or until thickened and bubbly. Spoon mixture into a serving dish; top with reserved sausage pieces. Serve immediately. Yield: 4 servings.

Note: Pumpernickel bread may be served with this dish.

KRAUT AND FRANKFURTER SKILLET

½ cup water
¼ cup butter or margarine
1 medium potato, peeled and cubed
1 medium apple, peeled, cored, and sliced
½ cup chopped onion
3 (16-ounce) cans shredded sauerkraut, drained
1 teaspoon sugar
1 teaspoon caraway seeds
¼ teaspoon pepper
1 pound cooked frankfurters, cut into 1-inch pieces

Combine water and butter in a large Dutch oven; cook over medium heat until butter melts. Add potato, apple, and onion; bring to a boil. Reduce heat; cover and simmer 15 minutes or until vegetables are tender.

Add sauerkraut, sugar, caraway seeds, and pepper; stir well. Bring to a boil. Reduce heat; cook, uncovered, over low heat 15 minutes or until liquid is absorbed. Stir in frankfurters. Cook over low heat 5 minutes or until frankfurters are thoroughly heated, stirring frequently. Spoon into a serving dish and serve immediately. Yield: 8 servings.

Klobase, Slovak for sausage, served with sauerkraut.

"Kansas City" was really the name of a sausage company located in New Orleans, in 1935.

The Historic New Orleans Collection, 533 Royal Street

CHICKEN-ANDOUILLE GUMBO

½ cup shortening
½ cup all-purpose flour
1 cup chopped onion
1 cup chopped celery
1 cup chopped green pepper
1 clove garlic, minced
1 (4- to 5-pound) baking hen, cut up
½ cup vegetable oil
6 cups water
1 pound andouille sausage, cut into ¼-inch slices
1 teaspoon salt
1 teaspoon pepper
½ teaspoon red pepper
Filé powder to taste
Hot cooked rice

Melt shortening in a large stockpot; stir in flour. Cook over medium heat, stirring occasionally, 10 minutes or until roux is the color of a copper penny. Add onion, celery, green pepper, and garlic; cook until vegetables are tender. Set aside.

Brown chicken in oil in a large skillet; drain, and set aside. Reserve drippings in skillet.

Add water to skillet, and bring to a boil. Remove from heat, and gradually pour pan dripping mixture over vegetable-flour mixture in stockpot, stirring constantly. Add chicken, sausage, salt, and pepper; cover and simmer 1 to 1½ hours, stirring occasionally. Remove from heat; stir in filé powder. Serve gumbo over rice. Yield: 5 quarts.

CHORIZO AND HOMINY SKILLET

2 tablespoons chopped onion
1 tablespoon butter or margarine
¾ pound Chorizo sausage, cut into ¼-inch-thick slices
2 tablespoons all-purpose flour
¼ teaspoon salt
Dash of pepper
1 (6-ounce) can evaporated milk
1 (16-ounce) can hominy, undrained
¼ cup chopped green pepper
2 tablespoons chopped green chiles
½ cup (2 ounces) shredded Cheddar cheese

Sauté onion in butter in a large skillet until tender; add sausage, and cook over medium heat until sausage is browned. Combine flour, salt, and pepper; add to skillet, stirring until smooth. Cook 1 minute, stirring constantly. Gradually add milk; cook over medium heat, stirring constantly, until thickened and bubbly.

Stir in hominy, green pepper, and chiles; cook over medium heat, stirring frequently, 10 minutes or until thickened and bubbly. Remove from heat, and sprinkle with cheese. Serve immediately. Yield: 4 servings.

BRATWURST IN SOUR CREAM SAUCE

2 (12-ounce) packages pre-cooked bratwurst
2 tablespoons butter or margarine
½ cup water
1 (8-ounce) carton commercial sour cream
1 tablespoon all-purpose flour
½ teaspoon salt

Fill a large Dutch oven half full of water; bring to a boil. Place bratwurst in boiling water; cover and remove from heat. Let stand 5 minutes. Drain well, and pat dry.

Melt butter in a heavy skillet over low heat; add bratwurst, and cook, turning frequently, until browned. Add ½ cup water; simmer, uncovered, 15 minutes. Slice bratwurst into ¼-inch pieces, and remove to a warm serving platter. Set skillet aside with pan drippings.

Combine sour cream, flour, and salt, stirring well. Add sour cream mixture to reserved pan drippings; stir until smooth. Cook over low heat, stirring constantly, 5 minutes, or until mixture is slightly thickened. Add bratwurst slices to sour cream sauce; cook over low heat until thoroughly heated. Serve immediately. Yield: 6 servings.

FROM HEAD TO TAIL

The distinction we now make between bacon and ham did not always pertain. Frequent references are to be found in old diaries and inventories to "hams of bacon." While we now think of "salt pork" as dry, salt-cured meat used chiefly for seasoning vegetables in the South, it is interesting to find a recipe for boiled salt pork in *The New Dixie Cookbook*, dated 1895. It starts like this: "Wash a piece of salt pork, *the leg is best*, put over the fire in cold water to cover and boil slowly three hours, allowing twenty minutes to the pound. . . . " The meat in question was not what we call bacon; it was ham.

"Breakfast bacon" was the term that separated the fatty salt- and/or smoke-cured seasoning meat from the side meat or "middling" with more streaks of lean in it. But tolerance for animal fat was higher then than now, and when the breakfast bacon gave out, the cook cheerfully sliced and fried her salt pork or jowl and served it with gravy and biscuits. Bacon was a blanket term for cured meat, whether ham, shoulder, middling, or jowl.

Canadian bacon is the pork equivalent of beef eye-of-round. Pork chop or T-bone steak may be envisioned, with the small tenderloin on one side of the bone, the larger round of meat on the other. It is the latter, whole, which becomes Canadian bacon from pork, eye-of-round from beef.

Many of the once-popular variety meats have dropped from favor in this century; few of us knowingly eat the ears and tail anymore. But Southerners still consume pork liver and liver dumplings, chitterlings or chit'lins, pig's feet, brains, and scrapple. Head cheese or souse, similar to the English "brawn," is still made on some farms and is available in commercial form.

When a Southerner remembers who he is, he inevitably knows the value of pork in his diet, no matter how sophisticated he becomes or how far he travels. He has been bred to want his turnip greens seasoned with ham hocks, his black-eyed peas with jowl bacon. This chapter is the story of what happens to all the small but indispensable parts of the hog after the fresh roasts are eaten and the hams are cured.

Fried Salt Pork with Mustard, Glazed Sweet Potatoes, and Turnip Greens are pictured at the Owens Spring Creek Farm Museum, at Richardson, Texas.

TEXAS SALT PORK SUPPER

A menu such as this may be thought of as a tribute to the settlers who pushed the frontier ahead of them and put down roots in strange, frequently hostile, new ground. It was a fact of pioneer life that a barrel or gunny sack of salt pork was a reliable, unspoilable ration whenever game could not be found and precious livestock had to be saved. As much a staple in the North as in the South, crisply fried salt pork went as well with boiled codfish as with Southern sweet potatoes and turnip greens. Texas cowpokes trailed with salt pork; now we have it for supper.

FRIED SALT PORK WITH MUSTARD
GLAZED SWEET POTATOES
TURNIP GREENS
BEER BREAD
PINEAPPLE MERINGUE PIE

Serves 6

Fannie Lou Spelce Associates

FRIED SALT PORK WITH MUSTARD

1 pound salt pork, cut in ¼-inch slices
Cornmeal
2 tablespoons vegetable oil
Prepared mustard

Place salt pork in a medium mixing bowl; add warm water to cover. Soak 1 hour; drain. Repeat soaking procedure.

Place salt pork in a large skillet; add water to cover. Bring to a boil; remove from heat, and drain. Plunge salt pork into cold water.

Dredge salt pork slices in cornmeal. Cook in oil in a large skillet over medium heat until crisp and brown, turning once. Drain well on paper towels. Serve hot with mustard. Yield: 6 servings.

GLAZED SWEET POTATOES

6 medium-size sweet potatoes
½ cup honey
⅓ cup orange juice
¼ cup butter or margarine
2 tablespoons lemon juice

Combine sweet potatoes and water to cover in a large Dutch oven. Bring to a boil. Reduce heat; cover and simmer 30 minutes or until tender. Drain and peel; slice potatoes lengthwise into ¼-inch-thick slices. Place potatoes in a large skillet, and set aside.

Combine remaining ingredients in a small saucepan. Bring to a boil; stir until butter melts. Remove from heat; pour honey mixture over potatoes. Cook, uncovered, over medium heat 20 minutes, basting often with honey mixture. Transfer potatoes to a warm serving platter; spoon honey mixture over potatoes. Serve immediately. Yield: 6 servings.

Busy Week at the Home Place *was painted by Fannie Lou Spelce, 1979.*

TURNIP GREENS

1 bunch (about 3 pounds) turnip greens
1 medium onion, chopped
1½ tablespoons vegetable oil
¾ teaspoon sugar
¾ teaspoon salt
½ teaspoon pepper
Hot sauce (optional)

Cut off and discard tough stems and discolored leaves from greens. Wash greens thoroughly in cold water several times; drain slightly. Set aside.

Sauté onion in oil in a large Dutch oven until tender. Add greens, sugar, salt, and pepper. Cover and cook over low heat, stirring occasionally, 1½ hours or until greens are tender. Serve with hot sauce, if desired. Yield: 6 servings.

BEER BREAD

3 cups self-rising flour
3 tablespoons sugar
1 (12-ounce) can beer

Combine all ingredients in a mixing bowl; mix well. Spoon into a greased 9- x 5- x 3-inch loafpan. Bake at 350° for 50 minutes or until a wooden pick inserted in center comes out clean. Cool 10 minutes in pan; remove to a wire rack, and cool completely. Bread may be sliced and toasted. Yield: 1 loaf.

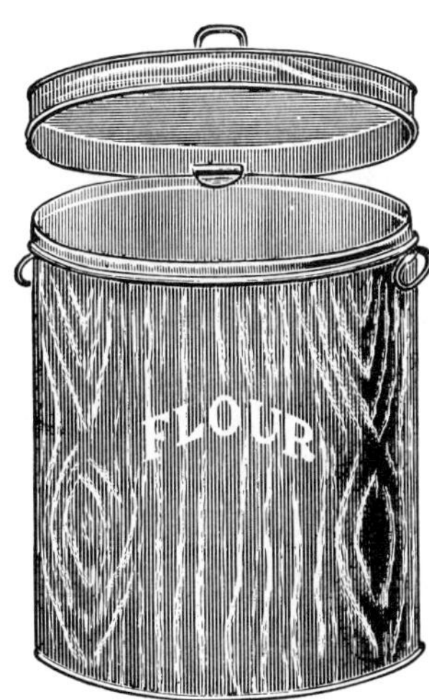

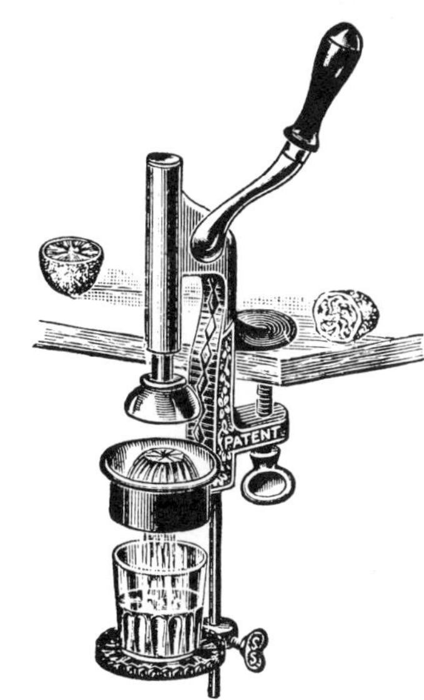

PINEAPPLE MERINGUE PIE

1¼ cups sugar
¼ cup plus 1 tablespoon cornstarch
2 tablespoons butter or margarine
1 teaspoon grated lemon rind
½ teaspoon salt
4 eggs, separated
2 cups boiling water
2 cups chopped fresh pineapple
3 tablespoons lemon juice
1 baked (9-inch) pastry shell
¼ teaspoon cream of tartar
¼ cup sugar

Combine 1¼ cups sugar, cornstarch, butter, lemon rind, salt, and egg yolks in a heavy saucepan; stir well. Pour boiling water over sugar mixture, stirring well. Cook over medium heat 5 minutes or until thickened and bubbly, stirring constantly. Remove from heat. Stir in pineapple and lemon juice. Pour filling into pastry shell.

Beat egg whites (at room temperature) and cream of tartar until foamy. Gradually add ¼ cup sugar, 1 tablespoon at a time, beating until stiff peaks form. Spread meringue over warm filling, sealing to edge of pastry. Bake at 350° for 10 to 12 minutes or until golden brown. Cool to room temperature. Yield: one 9-inch pie.

BACON: NOT JUST FOR BREAKFAST

FRIED BREAKFAST BACON WITH MILK GRAVY

6 slices bacon
1 tablespoon all-purpose flour
⅔ cup milk
⅛ teaspoon pepper

Cook bacon in a heavy skillet until crisp; remove bacon, reserving 1 tablespoon drippings in skillet. Drain bacon on paper towels; set aside.

Add flour to pan drippings in skillet; cook over medium heat, stirring constantly, until flour browns. Gradually add milk, stirring constantly, until thickened and bubbly. Stir in pepper. Serve hot gravy with bacon. Yield: 2 servings.

CARLYLE HOUSE FRIED APPLES AND BACON

1 pound bacon
4 medium-size cooking apples, peeled, cored, and cubed
1 tablespoon sugar

Cook bacon in a large heavy skillet. Drain bacon on paper towels; set aside. Reserve ¼ cup drippings in skillet.

Place apples in reserved bacon drippings in skillet, and sprinkle with sugar. Cover and cook over medium heat 15 minutes or until apples are tender. Uncover and cook an additional 15 minutes or until liquid has evaporated and apples have browned. Remove to a warm serving platter, and garnish with bacon. Serve immediately. Yield: 6 to 8 servings.

The meat locker of a butcher shop located near Mobile in Baldwin County, Alabama, c.1930.

BACON AND PIQUANT GREEN BEANS

½ pound smoked bacon, cut into ½-inch pieces
½ cup chopped onion
1 (16-ounce) can French-style green beans, drained
⅓ cup chili sauce

Cook bacon in a heavy skillet until crisp; remove bacon, reserving ¼ cup drippings in skillet. Drain bacon on paper towels; set aside.

Sauté onion in pan drippings over low heat until tender. Add green beans, chili sauce, and reserved bacon; stir well. Serve hot. Yield: 4 servings.

A charming recipe found in *The Cottage Kitchen*, 1883, directs the cook to cut thin slices of breakfast bacon and fry quickly; then take them up and fry round slices of firm apples, not too tart, and arrange them in a flat dish with the bacon all around. "A homely dish," the writer concludes, "but if cooked as directed, so good that you will be solicited to repeat the experiment once and again."

Mechanical apple parer looked odd, but worked like a charm.

Collection of Business Americana

BACON AND EGG SANDWICH SPREAD

6 slices bacon, cooked and crumbled
2 hard-cooked eggs, chopped
2 tablespoons sweet pickle relish
1 tablespoon mayonnaise
White bread slices

Combine bacon, egg, pickle relish, and mayonnaise in a small mixing bowl; mix well. Cover and chill until ready to use. Spread on bread slices to serve. Yield: about ¾ cup.

BAKED CANADIAN BACON WITH PORT WINE SAUCE

1½ cups firmly packed brown sugar
1 tablespoon cider vinegar
1 tablespoon prepared mustard
1 (4½- to 5-pound) whole Canadian bacon
1 cup Chablis or other dry white wine
Port Wine Sauce

Combine brown sugar, vinegar, and mustard in a medium mixing bowl, mixing to form a paste; stir well, and set aside.

Place bacon in a lightly greased roasting pan; coat with brown sugar paste. Cover tightly with aluminum foil, and refrigerate overnight.

Pour wine over bacon; cover and bake at 350° for 1½ hours. Uncover and bake an additional 30 minutes or until bacon has browned. Remove bacon to a warm serving platter; let stand 10 minutes before slicing. Slice and serve with Port Wine Sauce. Yield: 16 servings.

Port Wine Sauce:

1 cup red currant jelly
1 cup port wine
1 tablespoon butter or margarine

Combine all ingredients in a small saucepan. Cook, uncovered, over medium heat until thoroughly heated. Serve hot. Yield: 2 cups.

The bacon in this Memphis, Tennessee, meat shop, 1931, looks like a bargain until it is recalled that wages were comparably low.

Memphis Room, Memphis/Shelby County Public Library and Information Center

Baked Stuffed Canadian Bacon may be just the thing for that next dinner party.

BAKED STUFFED CANADIAN BACON

1 (5- to 5½-pound) whole Canadian bacon
6 cups soft breadcrumbs
1 medium onion, finely chopped
½ cup vinegar
1 egg, beaten
2 tablespoons sugar
1 tablespoon celery seeds
1 teaspoon dry mustard
1 teaspoon pepper
½ teaspoon red pepper
¼ cup sherry
2 teaspoons firmly packed brown sugar
1 teaspoon ground cloves

Place bacon in a well-greased shallow roasting pan. Cover tightly with aluminum foil. Bake at 325° for 2 hours.

Combine breadcrumbs and onion; stir in vinegar, egg, sugar, celery seeds, mustard, and pepper. Set aside.

Remove bacon from oven. Cut a horizontal pocket to within ½-inch of opposite side of bacon, slicing entire length of bacon. Carefully place stuffing mixture, end to end, inside bacon. Tie with string to secure. Return bacon to roasting pan.

Combine sherry, brown sugar, and cloves; stir well. Baste bacon with sherry mixture; set remaining mixture aside for basting purposes.

Bake bacon, uncovered, at 325° for 30 mintues or until browned, basting frequently with sherry mixture. Transfer to a warm serving platter. Let stand 10 minutes before slicing. Slice and serve with sherry sauce. Yield: 18 to 20 servings.

Pork is always killed before dawn, in order that, if possible, it may all be cut up the same day and put away without loss of time. Use Liverpool salt for curing it. Rub every piece well on the skin, in the first place . . . pack away in hogsheads with the skin downward, and let it remain untouched five or six weeks, according to the temperature of the weather. . . . Too long lying in salt makes bacon rusty. . . . Where the place is safe, bacon may be left hanging in the smokehouse all the year.

Virginia Cookery-Book, 1885

PORK AND BEANS

- 1 (16-ounce) package dried great Northern beans
- ½ pound salt pork, rinsed
- ½ cup molasses
- 2 tablespoons prepared mustard
- 3 cups boiling water

Sort and wash beans; place in a large Dutch oven. Cover with water 2 inches above beans; let soak overnight. Drain beans.

Combine beans, salt pork, and water to cover in Dutch oven. Bring to a boil. Reduce heat; cover, and simmer 30 minutes. Drain beans, and slice salt pork.

Place salt pork in bottom of a 3-quart casserole; stir in beans, molasses, and mustard. Add water; cover and bake at 350° for 2 hours. Uncover; bake for 45 minutes or until beans are tender and lightly browned. Yield: 6 to 8 servings.

A 1920s window display committed to memory the Van Camp name and can.

Birmingham Public Library Archives

Salt Pork and Potato Stew: Such a delicious dish to be made from very homely ingredients.

CREAMED SALT PORK OVER TOAST POINTS

½ pound salt pork, rinsed and ground
2 tablespoons all-purpose flour
2 cups milk
¼ teaspoon pepper
Toast points

Brown pork in a large skillet over medium heat; drain and set aside. Reserve 2 tablespoons drippings in skillet.

Add flour to skillet, stirring until smooth. Cook 2 to 3 minutes, stirring constantly. Gradually add milk; cook over medium heat, stirring constantly, until thickened and bubbly. Stir in reserved pork and pepper. Serve hot over toast points. Yield: 2 cups.

Note: Creamed Salt Pork may also be served over hot biscuits.

This advice from an 1895 recipe for fried salt pork: . . . While making gravy, place the fried pork where it will keep hot but not fry, as it should be sent to table in nice dry crisp slices without a particle of grease visible. An excellent way of serving is to dust with white pepper and turn a little sweet cream over the slices.

SALT PORK AND POTATO STEW

12 small red potatoes
¼ pound salt pork, chopped
2 cups water
¼ cup chopped onion
1 tablespoon chopped fresh parsley
¼ teaspoon pepper
½ cup hot milk
2 teaspoons all-purpose flour
Fresh parsley sprigs (optional)

Cook potatoes in boiling water 15 to 20 minutes or until tender; drain potatoes and let cool. Peel potatoes.

Combine potatoes, salt pork, water, onion, chopped parsley, and pepper in a small Dutch oven. Bring to a boil. Reduce heat; simmer, uncovered, 45 minutes.

Combine hot milk and flour, stirring until smooth. Add milk mixture to stew; cook over medium heat 5 minutes or until stew is slightly thickened. Garnish with fresh parsley sprigs, if desired. Serve immediately. Yield: 1 quart.

Dinner at May's Boarding House, *an oil on panel by Clara Williamson, dated 1954. Boarders saw lots of jowl and ham hocks.*

SALT PORK AND APPLES

- ½ pound salt pork, sliced
- 2 medium-size cooking apples, cored, peeled, and sliced into rings
- 2 tablespoons sugar
- ¼ teaspoon ground cinnamon

Fry pork in a large skillet over medium heat until browned and crisp. Drain pork on paper towels; set aside. Reserve 1 tablespoon drippings in skillet.

Fry apples in skillet until lightly browned and tender, turning once.

Place apples around pork on serving platter. Combine sugar and cinnamon; sprinkle over apples. Yield: 4 servings.

VEGETABLE HAMBONE SOUP

- 5 small potatoes, peeled and cubed
- 2 (10-ounce) packages frozen lima beans
- 1 (10-ounce) package frozen whole kernel corn
- 2 stalks celery, cut into 1-inch pieces
- 2 carrots, cut into 1-inch pieces
- 1 medium onion, chopped
- 1 quart tomato juice
- 1 ham bone
- 1 tablespoon sugar
- ½ teaspoon pepper
- ¼ teaspoon salt

Combine vegetables and water to cover in a Dutch oven. Bring to a boil. Reduce heat; cover and simmer 45 minutes. Add tomato juice, ham bone, and seasonings. Cover; simmer 1 hour. Yield: 5 quarts.

HAM HOCKS WITH CORNMEAL DUMPLINGS

- 2 pounds ham hocks
- 1 cup cornmeal
- ½ cup all-purpose flour
- 3 green onions, chopped
- ¾ teaspoon salt
- ¼ teaspoon pepper
- 1 egg, beaten

Combine ham hocks and water to cover in a large Dutch oven. Bring to a boil. Reduce heat; cover and simmer 1 hour.

Combine next 5 ingredients; mix well. Stir in 1 cup boiling ham hock broth. Add egg; mix well. Shape into 1½-inch dumplings. Drop dumplings into boiling ham broth; cover and cook 20 minutes. Remove dumplings from broth with a slotted spoon. Serve with ham hocks. Yield: 6 servings.

HAM HOCKS AND COLLARDS

1 bunch (about 3 pounds) collard greens
1 pound ham hocks
2 small red pepper pods
1 teaspoon salt
½ teaspoon pepper
Salt to taste (optional)

Cut off and discard tough stems and discolored leaves from greens. Wash greens thoroughly in cold water, changing the water several times; drain slightly.

Place collards, ham hocks, red pepper pods, 1 teaspoon salt, pepper, and water to cover in a large Dutch oven. Bring to a boil. Reduce heat; cover and simmer 3 hours or until greens are tender. Add water and salt to taste, if needed.

Remove greens from heat and drain, if necessary. Remove and discard pepper pods before serving. Yield: 6 to 8 servings.

Collard greens, like kale, are members of the cabbage family, one of the most popular in the South. Visitors to the South, however, have not always been convinced of the tastiness of greens or cabbage dishes. In the 1800s Frederick Olmstead found food at a "first class" hotel in Memphis "repulsive." The menu included no fewer than six cabbage dishes as well as "jole and greens."

TURNIP GREENS AND HOG JOWL

1 bunch (about 3 pounds) turnip greens
½ pound hog jowl
2 teaspoons salt
6 to 8 poached eggs (optional)
Cornbread (optional)

Cut off and discard tough stems and discolored leaves from greens. Wash greens thoroughly in cold water several times; drain slightly. Set aside.

Place hog jowl in a large Dutch oven; add water to cover. Bring to a boil; reduce heat, and simmer 45 minutes.

Add greens and salt; cook over low heat until steam begins to form. Reduce heat; cover and simmer, stirring occasionally, 1½ hours or until greens are tender. Add water, if needed.

Serve turnip greens and hog jowl with poached eggs and cornbread, if desired. Yield: 6 to 8 servings.

Auburn University home economics major feeds pig at 1948 hog show.

Auburn University Archives

Seasoned Pinto Beans (left) and Black-Eyed Peas and Hog Jowl are both very traditional.

BLACK-EYED PEAS AND HOG JOWL

1 cup dried black-eyed peas
3 cups water
2 small white onions, peeled
¼ pound hog jowl, cut into ½-inch cubes
1 teaspoon salt
¼ teaspoon pepper

Sort and wash peas; place in a medium Dutch oven. Cover with water 2 inches above peas; bring to a boil, and cook 5 minutes. Remove from heat; let stand 1 hour. Drain well.

Place peas, 3 cups water, onions, hog jowl, salt, and pepper in Dutch oven. Bring to a boil. Reduce heat; cover and simmer 1 hour or until peas are tender. Yield: 4 servings.

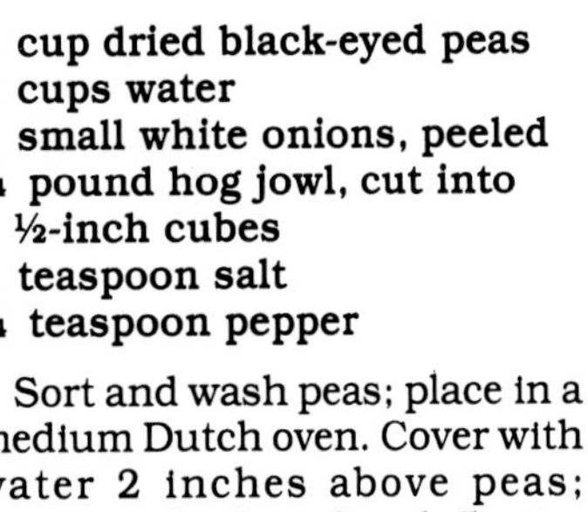

SEASONED PINTO BEANS

1½ cups dried pinto beans
¾ pound hog jowl, finely chopped
1½ cups finely chopped onion
1 cup finely chopped celery
½ cup finely chopped green pepper
½ teaspoon salt
1 cup regular rice, uncooked
Hot sauce (optional)

Sort and wash beans; place in a large Dutch oven. Cover with water 2 inches above beans; let soak overnight. Drain well.

Combine beans, hog jowl, onion, celery, green pepper, salt, and water to cover in Dutch oven. Bring to a boil. Reduce heat; cover and cook 2½ hours.

Drain cooking liquid from beans. Measure 2 cups cooking liquid; add back to beans. Discard remaining cooking liquid. (Water may be added to cooking liquid to equal 2 cups liquid, if needed.) Add rice, and stir well. Cover and cook over low heat 20 minutes or until liquid is absorbed. Serve with hot sauce, if desired. Yield: 8 to 10 servings.

There are a few culinary subjects which Southerners feel free to discuss only among themselves. One is jowl bacon, without which we'd be hard put to cook our dried beans and peas. Another is pot likker, the nectar obtained in no other way than by seasoning a mess of greens with jowl. There is little satisfaction to be had from talking vegetable cookery with our Northern friends; there is a difference in point of view. We come from people who laid on pork fat, butter, and cream in a profligate way; their heritage was more austere. Moral: Don't ask a Northerner whether he crumbles or dunks his cornbread into his pot likker.

BRAINS SCRAMBLED WITH EGGS

1 pound pork brains
1 small onion, chopped
3 tablespoons butter or margarine
6 eggs
1 teaspoon baking powder
½ teaspoon salt
¼ teaspoon pepper

Wash brains thoroughly in cold water; carefully remove membrane. Drain brains well, and chop.

Sauté brains and onion in butter in a large skillet until onion is tender. Combine eggs, baking powder, salt, and pepper; beat well, and stir into brains mixture. Cook over medium heat, stirring frequently, until eggs are firm but still moist. Serve immediately. Yield: 6 servings.

One of the fun chores: Looking for eggs in the barn. Photograph taken c.1875.

FRIED PIG'S FEET

4 pig's feet, cleaned and scraped
1 teaspoon salt
1⅓ cups all-purpose flour
½ teaspoon salt
¼ teaspoon pepper
¾ cup milk
2 egg yolks, beaten
Vegetable oil

Place pig's feet in a large container with cold water to cover. Soak 3 hours; scrub with a stiff brush. Rinse thoroughly.

Place pig's feet and 1 teaspoon salt in a large Dutch oven with water to cover. Bring to a boil. Reduce heat; cover and simmer 3 hours or until meat is tender and separates from bones. Remove pig's feet from cooking liquid with a slotted spoon; drain well. Set aside. Discard cooking liquid.

Combine flour, ½ teaspoon salt, and pepper in a medium bowl. Combine milk and yolks; add to flour mixture, mixing well to form a thick batter.

Dip pig's feet into batter, coating well. Fry in hot oil (375°) until golden brown. Drain on paper towels; serve immediately. Yield: 4 servings.

PICKLED PIG'S FEET

4 pig's feet, cleaned and scraped
1 small onion, thinly sliced
½ cup chopped celery
1 bay leaf
1 teaspoon salt
½ teaspoon pepper
1 cup cider vinegar
12 whole cloves
1 bay leaf

Place pig's feet in a large container with cold water to cover. Soak 3 hours; scrub with a stiff brush. Rinse thoroughly.

Combine pig's feet, onion, celery, 1 bay leaf, salt, and pepper in a large Dutch oven with cold water to cover. Bring to a boil. Reduce heat; cover and simmer 3 hours or until meat is tender and separates from bones. Remove feet from cooking liquid with a slotted spoon. Place in a plastic, glass, or stainless steel container with a tight-fitting lid; set aside.

Strain cooking liquid through a sieve; discard vegetables and bay leaf. Set cooking liquid aside to allow fat to rise to surface. Remove fat, and discard. Set cooking liquid aside.

Combine vinegar, cloves, and remaining bay leaf in a saucepan. Bring to a boil; reduce heat, and simmer 1 minute. Add reserved cooking liquid, and bring to a boil.

Pour vinegar mixture over pig's feet to completely cover. (Additional water may be added to cover pig's feet, if necessary.) Set aside to cool to room temperature. Cover and refrigerate 24 hours.

Remove pig's feet from vinegar mixture; serve cold. Yield: 4 servings.

SCRAPPLE

2 to 2½ pounds pig's feet
1 pound cubed lean pork
1 cup cornmeal
1 small onion, chopped
1 teaspoon salt
½ teaspoon rubbed sage
⅛ teaspoon pepper

Combine pig's feet, cubed pork, and water to cover in a large Dutch oven. Bring to a boil. Reduce heat; cover and simmer 2 hours or until meat is tender. Drain well, reserving 4 cups broth.

Remove meat from pig's feet; discard bones. Combine pig's feet meat and cubed pork; grind together using coarse blade of meat grinder. Set ground pork mixture aside.

Strain reserved broth into top of a double boiler. Place over boiling water; add cornmeal, and cook over boiling water 5 minutes, stirring constantly. Add ground pork mixture, onion, salt, sage, and pepper; stir well. Cook over boiling water 1 hour, stirring occasionally. Spoon mixture into a lightly greased 8½- x 4½- x 3-inch loafpan. Cover and refrigerate several hours or until set. Cut into thin slices, and serve cold. Yield: one 8½-inch loaf.

Note: Scrapple may be sliced thin, and pan fried until browned, if desired.

Living High, Low, and Middle on the Hog, *by Mississippian Alice Moseley, 1970s.*

Alice Latimer Moseley

HEAD CHEESE

1 pig's head, cleaned and scraped
4 pig's feet, cleaned and scraped
1 medium onion, finely chopped
1 cup cider vinegar
2 tablespoons rubbed sage
1 tablespoon salt
2 tablespoons red pepper flakes
Hot sauce
Saltine crackers

Place pig's head and feet in a large stockpot with cold water to cover. Soak 3 hours; scrub with a stiff brush. Scrape thoroughly, especially the ears, to remove all bristle. Rinse. Set pig's feet aside.

Cut head into four pieces with a meat saw. Scrub tongue with a stiff brush. Remove eyes; discard. Remove brain; reserve for use in other recipes. Rinse head thoroughly.

Place pig's head and feet in a large stockpot with water to cover. (Two stockpots may be required if head is large.) Bring to a boil. Reduce heat; cover and simmer 4 hours or until meat begins to fall from bones. Skim froth occasionally from top of cooking liquid; discard.

Remove stockpot from heat; set aside. Allow meat to cool completely in liquid. Remove head and feet from cooking liquid. Drain; remove meat from bones. Set meat aside. Reserve 2 cups cooking liquid.

Grind meat into a large mixing bowl using coarse blade of meat grinder. Add reserved cooking liquid and remaining ingredients, mixing well.

Press meat mixture firmly into 6 waxed paper lined 7½- 3- x 2-inch loafpans. Cover tightly, and refrigerate 3 to 4 days to blend seasonings.

Remove head cheese from loafpans. Remove waxed paper. Wrap tightly in plastic wrap, and store in refrigerator for up to 3 months.

Cut into thin slices, and serve cold with hot sauce and crackers. Yield: 6 loaves.

Head Cheese, to serve in thin slices with crackers.

Head cheese is sometimes called souse because it contains vinegar to "pickle" or preserve it. Marion Harland wrote, "This is generally eaten cold for tea, with vinegar and mustard, but it is very nice cut in slices, seasoned slightly with mustard, and warmed in a frying pan with enough butter to prevent burning. Or, you may dip in beaten egg, then cracker-crumbs, and fry for breakfast. . . . " She also suggested that it was nice to use an iron pig's head form, as shown above, for molding head cheese.

GERMAN PANNAS

3 cups pig's head meat
3 cups broth from cooked meat
1½ teaspoons salt
½ teaspoon pepper
1½ cups cornmeal
½ cup all-purpose flour
Vegetable oil

Combine meat, broth, salt, and pepper in a large Dutch oven. Bring to a boil. Reduce heat. Stir in remaining ingredients, except oil; mix well. Cook, uncovered, over low heat 15 minutes, stirring constantly. Remove from heat, and pour into a large shallow baking dish; pack firmly into dish. Cool slightly; refrigerate until chilled.

Cut mixture into ½-inch-thick slices; fry in hot oil in a large heavy skillet until golden brown on both sides. Drain. Serve hot as a breakfast dish. Yield: 15 to 20 servings.

CAJUN LIVER PÂTÉ

1 pound ground pork liver
¾ pound ground pork
½ pound ground pork fat
2 small cloves garlic, minced
2½ teaspoons salt
1 teaspoon pepper
¾ teaspoon red pepper

Combine all ingredients in a large mixing bowl; mix well. Place in a large Dutch oven with water to cover.

Cook, uncovered, over medium heat, stirring often, 1½ hours or until fat rises to top.

Pour mixture into jars; cover with metal lids, and screw bands tight. Refrigerate 24 hours. (Fat will rise to top of jars to help seal pâté.)

Let pâté come to room temperature. Remove band and lid from jar. Stir pâté well to distribute fat throughout mixture. Spread on crackers or French bread. Yield: 3 pints.

LIVER DUMPLINGS

1 large onion, chopped
¼ cup butter or margarine, melted
1½ pounds pork liver, finely chopped
4 cups soft breadcrumbs
2 eggs, beaten
2 tablespoons all-purpose flour
½ teaspoon salt
4 cups beef broth

Sauté onion in butter until tender. Combine onion, liver, breadcrumbs, eggs, flour, and salt in a medium mixing bowl; stir until well blended.

Bring broth to a boil in a small Dutch oven. Drop liver mixture by teaspoonfuls into boiling broth. Reduce heat; cover and simmer 30 minutes. Remove dumplings with a slotted spoon to a warm platter; discard cooking liquid. Serve immediately. Yield: 6 to 8 servings.

A 1919 picture of the Boys Pig Club, Auburn, Alabama. Extension agent sits at right.

Auburn University Archives

THE BARNUM & BAILEY
GREATEST
SHOW
ON EARTH

"HOME SWEET HOME."

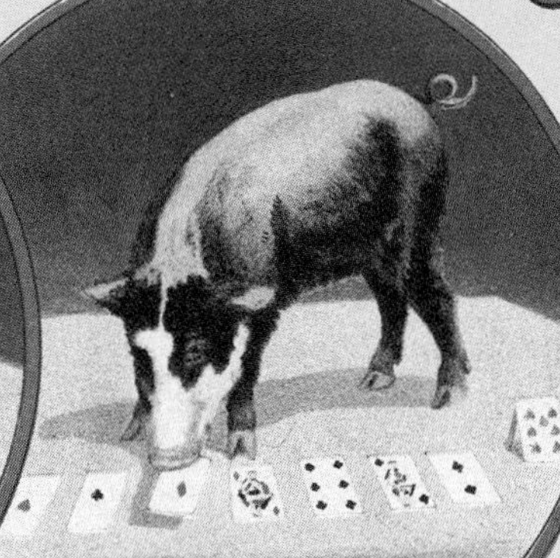

THE RIGHT CARD.

"GOD SAVE THE QUEEN."
"YANKEE-DOODLE"
TROUPE OF VERY REMARKABLE TRAINED PIGS.

CUTS OF PORK

Cubed Steak
Pork Cubes
— Braise, Cook in Liquid, — Broil
② Blade Steak
Braise, Panfry
② Smoked Shoulder Roll
Roast (Bake), Cook in Liquid
① Blade Chop
② Rib Chop
② Loin Chop
③ Sirloin Chop
Cubed Steak
②③ Butterfly Chop
② Top Loin Chop
③ Sirloin Cutlet
Braise, Broil, Panbroil, Panfry

①②③ Boneless Leg (Fresh Ham)
Roast
①②③ Sliced Cooked "Boiled" Ham
Heat or Serve Cold
①②③ Boneless Smoked Ham
①②③ Canned Ham
Roast (Bake)
② Boneless Smoked Ham Slices
② Center Smoked Ham Slice
Broil, Panbroil, Panfry
①② Smoked Ham, Rump (Butt) Portion
③ Smoked Ham, Shank Portion
Roast (Bake), Cook in Liquid

② Boneless Blade Boston Roast
② Blade Boston Roast
— Braise, Roast —

④ Fat Back
Panfry, Cook in Liquid
①④ Lard
Pastry, Cookies, Quick Breads, Cakes, Frying

① Country-Style Ribs
①② Back Ribs
Roast (Bake), Braise, Cook in Liquid
② Smoked Loin Chop
①②③ Canadian-Style Bacon
Roast (Bake), Broil, Panbroil, Panfry
①②③ Boneless Top Loin Roast
①②③ Boneless Top Loin Roast
Roast
②③④ Tenderloin
Roast (Bake), Braise, Panfry
① Blade Loin
② Center Loin
③ Sirloin
Roast

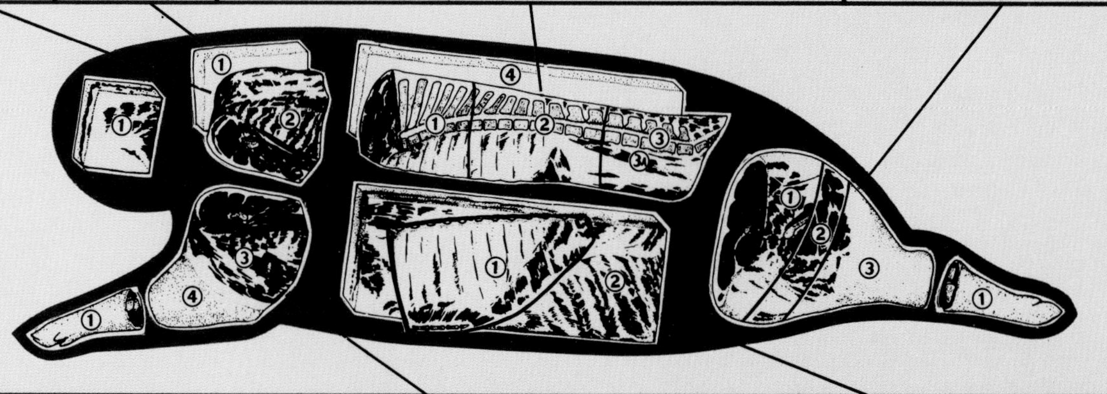

BOSTON SHOULDER
① CLEAR PLATE
④ FAT BACK
LOIN
LEG (FRESH OR SMOKED HAM)
JOWL
PICNIC SHOULDER
① SPARERIBS ② BACON (SIDE PORK)

① Smoked Jowl
Cook in Liquid, Broil, Panbroil, Panfry
① Pig's Feet
Cook in Liquid, Braise
③④ Fresh Arm Picnic
Roast
③④ Smoked Arm Picnic
Roast (Bake), Cook in Liquid
③ Arm Roast
Roast
Ground Pork
Roast (Bake), Panbroil, Panfry
Fresh Hock
Smoked Hock
Braise, Cook in Liquid
②③ Neck Bones
Cook in Liquid
③ Arm Steak
Braise, Panfry
Link
Roll
Sausage
Panfry, Braise, Bake
① Spareribs
② Slab Bacon
① Salt Pork
Bake, Broil, Panbroil, Panfry, Cook in Liquid
② Sliced Bacon
Bake, Broil, Panbroil, Panfry

GOOD TO KNOW

SELECTING QUALITY PORK

Pork varies in tenderness according to the cut; however, most pork cuts can be made tender by proper cooking. When selecting a cut of pork, keep the cooking method in mind. Consider not only the size and cut, but also the quality of the pork.

- Pork is graded according to general conformation, marbling or quality associated with tenderness, juiciness, flavor, and the amount of usable meat.
- Check the pork for freshness and quality before purchasing. Read the label to determine the grade, cut, and weight.
- Usually pork costs less per pound when a large cut of pork, like a ham or loin, is purchased. The butcher can then cut the pork to your specifications.
- The more difficult the pork is to carve and the more bone there is in relation to the lean, the less expensive the cut.

PURCHASING

When selecting a cut of pork, consider the cost per serving instead of the cost per pound. Bone, gristle, and fat in a cut of pork can reduce the actual number of servings per pound.

- Boneless pork: allow ¼ to ⅓ pound per serving (tenderloin, ground pork, boneless roasts and ham)
- Bone-in pork: allow ⅓ to ½ pound per serving (chops, steaks, roasts, ham)
- Bony meat: allow ¾ to 1 pound per serving (spareribs, country-style ribs, hocks)

PORK PURCHASING GUIDE

Type	Retail Cut	Servings Per Pound*
Roasts	Leg, bone-in	3
	Leg, boneless	3½
	Rolled Top Loin, boneless	3½
	Center Loin	2½
	Blade Loin	3
	Smoked Loin	3
	Sirloin	2
	Rolled Blade Shoulder, boneless	3
	Arm Picnic Shoulder, bone-in	2
	Smoked Shoulder Roll	3
	Whole Tenderloin	4
Hams	Smoked Ham, bone-in	3½
	Smoked Ham, boneless	5
	Smoked Ham, canned	5
	Smoked Ham center slice	5
Chops and Steaks	Loin Chops	4
	Rib Chops	4
	Blade Chops or Steaks	3
	Boneless Chops	4
	Tenderloin Fillets	4
Ribs	Back Ribs	1½
	Country-style Back Ribs	1½
	Spareribs	1½
Other Cuts	Cubed or Ground Pork	1½
	Regular Bacon, sliced	6
	Canadian-style Bacon	5
	Hocks	1½
	Sausage	4

*Servings per pound based on an average serving of 2½ to 3½ ounces per portion.

REFRIGERATING AND FREEZING

Fresh pork is perishable and must be wrapped properly and stored at a safe temperature. The cut of pork determines the length of time it may be refrigerated or frozen.

Pork should always be stored in the coldest part of the refrigerator at temperatures between 32° and 40°F.

Prepackaged pork should be stored, unopened, in the original store wrapper. Unnecessary handling may contaminate the meat. Fresh unpackaged pork should be wrapped loosely in waxed paper or aluminum foil and placed in the refrigerator so that air can circulate around the package.

Never wash fresh pork before refrigerating since moisture encourages bacteria growth. Wipe with a damp cloth and/or scrape with the dull edge of a knife before cooking.

Smoked pork, sausage, ready-to-serve pork, and canned pork should be refrigerated in the original wrappings or containers. Country-cured hams may be refrigerated if tightly wrapped or hung in a cool, dry, well-ventilated place.

Leftover cooked pork should be cooled and tightly covered before refrigerating. Cooked pork should not stand at room temperature more than two hours before refrigerating.

Prepackaged pork may be frozen for 1 week without rewrapping. For longer freezer storage, the original package should be overwrapped with freezer wrapping material. Allow space around each package for good air circulation. Fresh pork should be wrapped with special moisture-proof, vapor-proof freezer wrapping material.

Never season or salt pork before freezing since many seasonings will intensify in flavor when frozen. Salt tends to draw moisture to the surface of meat, making it less juicy.

Smoked and cured cuts of pork should not be frozen for long periods of time. Canned hams should be removed from the can and wrapped in freezer wrapping paper before freezing.

Frozen pork should be thawed in the refrigerator before removing freezer wrappings. Additional cooking time should be allowed if pork is to be cooked without thawing.

Pork which has been frozen and thawed should be used immediately. Thawed pork should never be refrozen since refreezing can dry out the pork and affect its flavor.

A busy day at The Farmers' Market, Baltimore, Maryland, c.1930.

CARVING PORK

Carving pork properly is not difficult if certain necessities are observed: good sharp knives, a suitable cutting surface, and a knowledge about the cut to be carved.

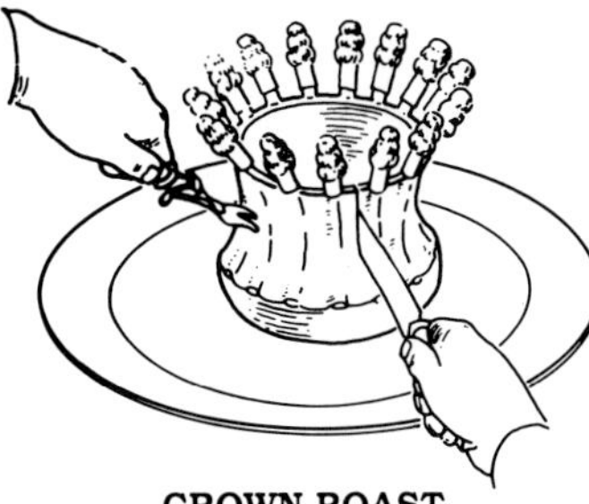

CROWN ROAST

Remove the stuffing from the center of the roast, if desired. Using a fork to secure the roast, slice down between the ribs and remove one chop at a time.

PORK LOIN

Remove the backbone before carving the roast. Cut close to the bone, leaving as much meat on the roast as possible. Arrange roast on platter with lean side of ribs facing carver.

Secure roast with a fork. Slice down both sides of each rib close to the bone. One slice will contain a rib bone and one slice will be boneless.

WHOLE HAM

Place ham on cutting surface, fat side up and shank to the carver's right. Cut away several lengthwise slices from the thin side of ham to form a solid base on which to rest the ham.

Turn ham on its base. Cut vertical slices down to the leg bone. Turn knife and cut horizontally along leg bone to remove slices.

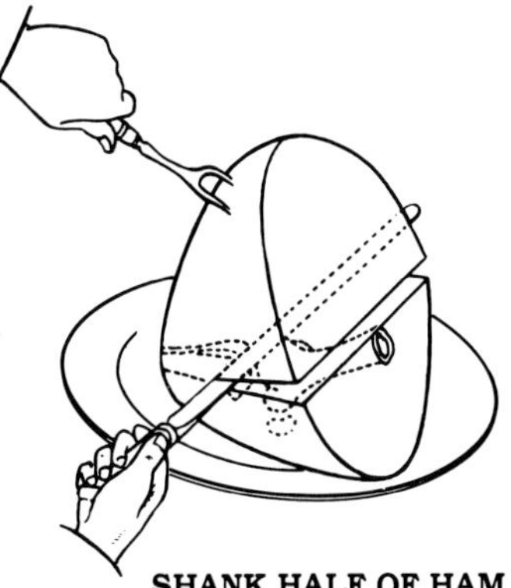

SHANK HALF OF HAM

Place ham on cutting surface to the carver's left, with the thick cushion of meat on top. Secure ham with a fork, and cut along the top of leg and shank bones and under fork. Remove the thick cushion of meat and place onto a cutting surface with the broadest side down.

Make perpendicular cuts down through the cushion of meat. Transfer cut slices of meat to a serving platter.

To remove meat from the remaining shank, cut around leg bone with tip of knife. Turn meat so that the broadest side is down. Slice meat the same way as was done in the previous step.

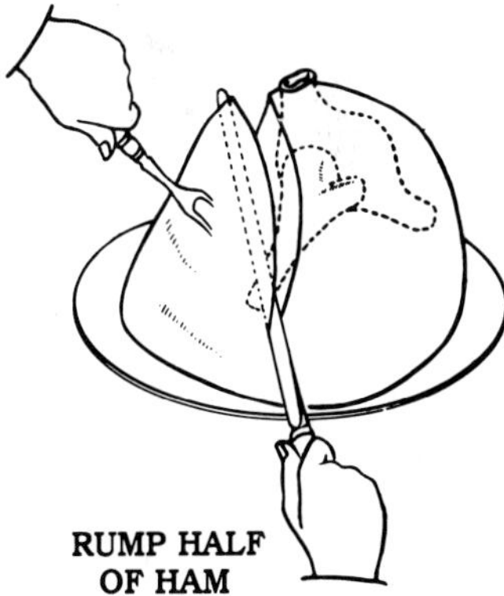

RUMP HALF OF HAM

Place rump half on cutting surface, cut side down. Cut down along hip bone to remove boneless portion of meat from the side. This portion may be from either side of the bone depending on whether the ham is from the right or left leg.

Place boneless portion on cutting surface, cut side down. Slice across the grain.

Securing the remaining rump with a fork, make horizontal slices across the meat to the hip bone. With the knife tip, cut each slice from bone, and remove to a serving platter.

RECOMMENDED COOKING METHODS, TIMES, AND TEMPERATURES FOR PORK

Cooking Method	Type	Cut	Approx. Thickness or Weight in Pounds	Approx. Cooking Time per Pound	Final Internal Temperature
ROASTING (300°F to 350°F)	**Fresh**	Loin			
		Center	3 to 5	30 to 35 min.	170°F
		Half	5 to 7	35 to 40 min.	170°F
		Blade loin or Sirloin	3 to 4	40 to 45 min.	170°F
		Top (double)	3 to 5	35 to 40 min.	170°F
		Crown	6 to 10	25 to 30 min.	170°F
		Arm Picnic Shoulder			
		Bone-in	5 to 8	30 to 35 min.	170°F
		Arm Roast	3 to 5	30 to 35 min.	170°F
		Blade Boston Shoulder	4 to 6	40 to 45 min.	170°F
		Leg (fresh ham)			
		Whole (bone-in)	14 to 16	22 to 24 min.	170°F
		Whole (boneless)	10 to 14	24 to 28 min.	170°F
		Half (bone-in)	7 to 8	35 to 40 min.	170°F
		Tenderloin	½ to 1	45 to 60 min.	170°F
		Ribs		1½ to 2 hrs.	Well done
	Smoked	Ham (fully cooked)			
		Whole (boneless)	8 to 12	15 to 18	140°F
		Half (boneless)	4 to 6	18 to 25	
		Ham (fully cooked)			
		Whole (bone-in)	14 to 16	15 to 18	130°F to
		Half (bone-in)	7 to 8	18 to 25	140°F
		Ham (cook-before-eating)			
		Whole (boneless)	8 to 12	17 to 21	160°F
		Ham (cook-before-eating)			
		Whole (bone-in)	14 to 16	18 to 20	160°F
		Half (bone-in)	7 to 8	22 to 25	160°F
		Loin	3 to 5	20 to 25	140°F
		Arm Picnic Shoulder (fully cooked)	5 to 8	25 to 30	140°F
		Arm Picnic Shoulder (cook-before-eating)	5 to 8	30 to 35	170°F
		Shoulder Roll (butt)	2 to 3	35 to 40	170°F
		Canadian-style Bacon (fully cooked)	2 to 4	20 to 30	140°F

Cooking Method	Type	Cut	Thickness	Total Cooking Time
BROILING (350°F to 400°F	**Fresh**	Chops	¾ to 1½ in.	30 to 45 min.
		Shoulder Steaks	½ to ¾ in.	30 to 45 min.
		Ribs		1 to 1½ hrs.
	Smoked	Ham Slice	½ in.	10 to 12 min.
		Loin Chops	½ to 1 in.	15 to 20 min.
		Canadian-style Bacon (sliced)	½ in.	6 to 8 min.
BRAISING	**Fresh**	Chops, fresh	¾ to 1½ in.	45 to 60 min.
		Ribs		1½ hrs.
		Tenderloin		
		Whole	½ to 1 in.	45 to 60 min.
		Slices	½ in.	30 min.
COOKING IN LIQUID	**Fresh**	Ribs		2 to 2½ hrs.
	Smoked	Ham, Country	10 to 16	4½ to 5 hrs.
		Half	5 to 8	3 to 4 hrs.
		Arm Picnic Shoulder	5 to 8	3½ to 4 hrs.

RECOMMENDED COOKING METHODS

Any cut of pork can be made tender, palatable, and flavorful if appropriate cooking methods are used. Most pork cuts can be cooked using several different cooking methods. Tender cuts use dry heat methods while less tender cuts require cooking with moist heat. The large roasts (loins, legs, shoulders) should be roasted or baked. Steaks can be pan fried or braised. Chops, cutlets, and ground pork can be braised, broiled, grilled, pan broiled, or pan fried. Ribs can be roasted, baked, broiled, or cooked in some kind of liquid.

DRY HEAT

Roasting: To roast means to cook by dry heat in an oven without liquid. This is best for large, tender cuts of meat.

Place the meat, fat side up, on a rack in a shallow roasting pan. The fat self-bastes the meat during cooking. Insert a meat thermometer so that the bulb rests in muscle tissue, not in fat or against bone. Do not cover. Cook until the meat reaches the desired degree of doneness or until the thermometer registers the recommended temperature.

Broiling: To broil means to cook by direct heat in an oven.

Set the oven on broil. Depending on the thickness of the cut, place the meat 2 to 5 inches from the broiler element. Steaks and patties that are ¾ to 1 inch thick need to be 2 to 3 inches from the element; larger cuts from 1 to 2 inches thick should cook 3 to 5 inches from the heat source. Broil until the top browns; the meat should be about half-done at this point. Season with salt now. (Do not salt before cooking because salt draws out the moisture and inhibits browning of the meat.)

Pan Broiling: To pan broil is to cook by direct heat in a pan. This method is used for cooking the same cuts that may be broiled, but the cooking is done in a frying pan or griddle on top of the stove, not in the oven.

When pan broiling, do not add fat or water to the skillet unless the cut is extremely lean and a bit of fat is needed to prevent sticking. Cook slowly over medium low heat, turning occasionally to make sure that the meat browns evenly. Pour fat from pan as it accumulates.

Frying: Fried meats are cooked in oil over medium heat. For pan frying, use a small amount of oil; for deep fat frying, use enough oil to completely cover the meat. Pan frying is best for tender meat such as cubed pork steak that has been tenderized by pounding.

Heat oil over medium heat. When hot, add the meat and brown. Do not cover the skillet because the meat will lose its crispness. Continue to cook on medium heat until done, turning occasionally. Remove from pan, and serve. During cooking, if the fat begins to smoke, lower the heat immediately.

MOIST HEAT

Braising: Braised meats are cooked slowly in a small amount of liquid. The slow cooking and moisture from the liquid are vital for tenderizing tough cuts of meat.

Brown the meat in a small amount of fat; then pour off the pan drippings. The browning adds flavor and improves the appearance. Season the meat; add a small amount of liquid such as water, tomato juice, or soup. Cover tightly, and simmer until tender. Depending on the size of the cut, braising can take 1 to 4 hours. Gravy may be made with the pan drippings.

Cooking in Liquid: To cook in liquid, cover the meat completely with water or other liquid.

Brown the meat; cover with water, and add seasonings. Cover with a lid, and simmer gently until tender. Boiling tends to toughen the meat and increases shrinkage. If vegetables are to be cooked with the meat, add them near the end of the cooking time.

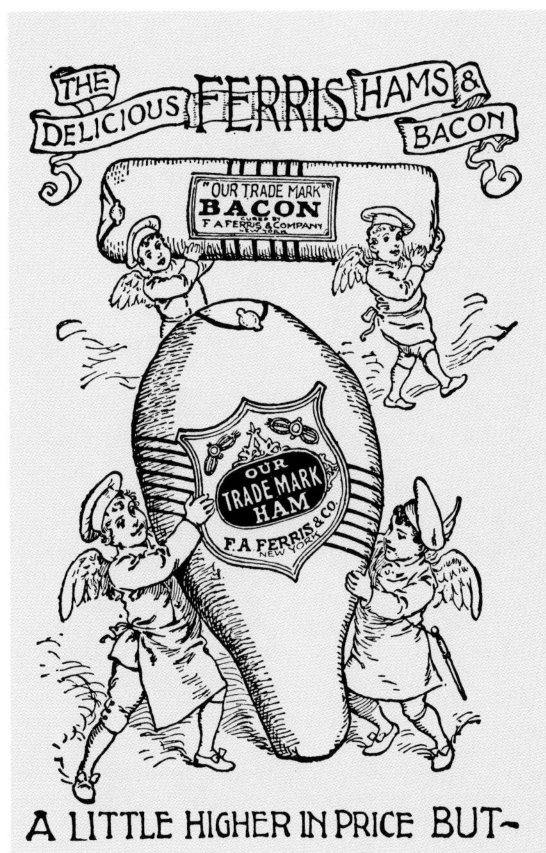

ACKNOWLEDGMENTS

Apple-Sausage Loaf, Baked Ham with Pickled Peaches, Ham Rolls, Ham Soufflé, Liver Dumplings adapted from *The South Carolina Cook Book*, collected and edited by the South Carolina Extension Homemakers Council and the Clemson Extension Home Economics Staff, ©1954. By permission of University of South Carolina Press, Columbia, South Carolina.

Arkansas Leg of Pork courtesy of Mrs. W.A. Rucker, Pine Bluff, Arkansas.

Bacon and Piquant Green Beans, Ham Croquettes, Ham Stew, Ham Turnovers, Smithfield Ham Biscuits, Vegetable Hambone Soup adapted from *The Smithfield Cookbook* by The Junior Woman's Club, ©1978. By permission of The Junior Woman's Club, Smithfield, Virginia.

Baked Canadian Bacon with Port Wine Sauce, Corny Dogs, Creole Jambalaya, Sausage Sauce Piquant, Stuffed Bell Peppers with Ham adapted from *Talk About Good!* by The Junior League of Lafayette, ©1969. By permission of The Junior League of Lafayette, Louisiana.

Baked Ham Salad, Ham Jambalaya, Mississippi Stuffed Ham, Savory Ham-Veal Ring adapted from *The Gasparilla Cookbook* by The Junior League of Tampa, ©1961. By permission of The Junior League of Tampa, Florida.

Baked Ham with Orange Glaze, Florida Barbecued Country-Style Ribs adapted from *Jane Nickerson's Florida Cookbook* ©1973. By permission of University Presses of Florida, Gainesville.

Baked Ham with Sauce adapted from *Jesse's Book of Creole and Deep South Recipes* by Edith Ballard Watts and John Watts. Published by Weathervane Books, 1954.

Baked Peanut Ham with Sherry adapted from *Cross Creek Cookery* by Marjorie Kinnan Rawlings, ©1942; copyright renewed 1970 by Norton Baskin. Permission of Charles Scribner's Sons, New York.

Barbecued Ham Steaks adapted from *Savannah: Proud as a Peacock* by The Savannah Junior Auxiliary, ©1981. By permission of The Savannah Junior Auxiliary, Savannah, Tennessee.

Barbecued Leg of Pork, Country-Pride Pork Chops, Grilled Pork Chops, Marinated Pork Steaks, Pork Roast Supreme, Southern Tender Kabobs, Special Pork Loin Roast adapted from *Cooking Today's Pork*.

Barbecued Whole Pig, Carolina Basting Sauce prepared for photography by Mr. Jim Elder and Mr. Willis Peaden, Havelock, North Carolina.

Bonaventure Barbecue Sauce, Kehoe Horseradish Sauce, Macaroni and Cheese with Ham, Savannah's Famous Fried Rice adapted from *Savannah Sampler Cookbook* by Margaret Wayt DeBolt, ©1978. By permission of The Donning Company/Publishers, Norfolk, Virginia.

Brains Scrambled with Eggs, Bratwurst in Sour Cream Sauce adapted from *Guten Appetit!* by The Sophienburg Museum, ©1978. By permission of The Sophienburg Museum, New Braunfels, Texas.

Carlyle House Fried Apples and Bacon adapted from *The Presidents' Cookbook* by Poppy Cannon and Patricia Brooks, ©1968. By permission of Funk and Wagnalls, New York.

Carolina Brunswick Stew prepared for photography by Alice Underhill, New Bern, North Carolina.

Chicken-Andouille Gumbo, Chicken-Sausage Jambalaya, Cajun Liver Pâté, Pork Steak Fricassee, Pork Rib Jambalaya adapted from *Acadiana Profile's Cajun Cooking*, edited by Trent Angers and Sue McDonough, ©1980. By permission of Angers Publishing Company, Lafayette, Louisiana.

Country Ham Cooked with a Blanket adapted from *Recipes from the Old South* by Martha Meade, ©1961. By permission of Holt, Rhinehart, and Winston, New York.

Country-Style Ribs courtesy of Mrs. James W. Edwards, Grove Hill, Alabama.

Creamed Salt Pork over Toast Points adapted from *Aunt Hank's Rock House Kitchen*, compiled by Georgia Mae Smith Ericson. By permission of Crosby County Pioneer Memorial Museum, Crosbyton, Texas.

Crown Roast of Pork with Sausage Stuffing, Kentucky Pork Sausage adapted from *Out of Kentucky Kitchens* by Marion Flexner, ©1949. By permission of Franklin Watts, Inc., New York.

Fried Pig's Feet, Head Cheese, Pickled Pig's Feet prepared by Mr. Deery Eakin, Shelbyville, Tennessee.

German Pannas adapted from *The Melting Pot: Ethnic Cuisine in Texas* by The Institute of Texan Cultures, ©1977. By permission of The University of Texas Institute of Texan Cultures, San Antonio, Texas.

Greek Cabbage Rolls, Klobase adapted from *It's Greek to Me* by Philoptochos Society of Annunciation Greek Orthodox Church, ©1981. By permission of Annunciation Greek Orthodox Church, Memphis, Tennessee.

Grilled Polish Sausage and Cabbage adapted from *Pork's Great Outdoors* by the National Live Stock and Meat Board, Chicago, Illinois.

Ham and Mushroom à la King, Pork Tenderloin with Prunes, Sweet-and-Sour Pork adapted from *Southern*

Sideboards by The Junior League of Jackson, ©1978. By permission of The Junior League of Jackson, Mississippi.

Ham Hocks and Collards, Pork Tenderloin with Sherried Apple Rings, Stuffed Baked Spareribs, Toad-in-the-Hole adapted from *Maryland's Way* by Mrs. Lewis R. Andrews and Mrs. J. Reaney Kelly. By permission of the Hammond-Harwood House Association, Annapolis, Maryland.

Ham Hocks with Cornmeal Dumplings, Grilled Pork Chops, Pork Steak with Raisin Dressing adapted from *The Mississippi Cookbook*, compiled by the Home Economics Division of the Mississippi Cooperative Extension Service. By permission of University Press of Mississippi, Jackson, Mississippi.

Ham Steak with Orange-Rice Stuffing, Roast Loin of Pork with Vegetables adapted from *The Jackson Cookbook* by the Symphony League of Jackson. By permission of the Symphony League of Jackson, Mississippi.

Hog's head, feet, and chitterlings provided by Mr. Jeff Nejmanowski of Rainbow Meat Packers, Lewisburg, Tennessee.

Honey Pork Chops adapted from *A Man's Taste* by the Junior League of Memphis, ©1980. By permission of the Junior League of Memphis, Tennessee.

Kielbasa adapted from *Prairie Harvest* by St. Peter's Episcopal Churchwomen, Tollville, Arkansas. By permission of St. Peter's Episcopal Churchwomen, Hazen, Arkansas.

Lemon Charlotte Russe adapted from *Georgia Heritage - Treasured Recipes*, ©1979. By permission of The National Society of The Colonial Dames of America in the State of Georgia, Huntsville, Georgia. Prepared for photography by Betty Douglas, Portsmouth, Virginia.

Louisiana-Style Pork Roast adapted from the collection of National Pork Producers Council.

Meat for photograph on page 6 smoked and furnished by Uncle Mort's Restaurant, Jasper, Alabama.

Montezuma Pie adapted from *On-the-Border, By-the-Sea* by the Church of the Advent, ©1975. By permission of Church of the Advent, Brownsville, Texas.

Mustard Cole Slaw prepared for photography by Betty Colby, New Bern, North Carolina.

Owens Sausage Stew courtesy of Owens Country Sausage, Owens Spring Creek Farm, Richardson, Texas.

Pigs for Barbecued Whole Pig and Roast Suckling Pig courtesy of North Carolina Pork Producer's Association, Raleigh, North Carolina.

Pork Chops in Vermouth adapted from *The Monticello Cookbook* by The University of Virginia Hospital Circle, ©1950. By permission of The Uinversity Virginia of Virginia Hospital Circle, Charlottesville, Virginia.

Pork Chop Suey courtesy of Mrs. Carolyn Jones, Tuscumbia, Alabama.

Red Beans and Rice adapted from *The Plantation Cookbook* by The Junior League of New Orleans, ©1972. By permission of Doubleday and Company, Inc., New York.

Roast Suckling Pig prepared by Elaine Harvell, North Carolina Pork Producers Association, Raleigh, North Carolina.

Sauer-Beckman Bratwurst courtesy of Mr. Donald W. Schuch, Park Superintendent, LBJ State Historical Park, Stonewall, Texas.

Sausage-Cheese Dip courtesy of Mrs. David Owen, Sheffield, Alabama.

Sherried Spareribs adapted from *Green Springs Country Cooking*, by Members of Historic Green Springs, Inc., ©1975. By permission of The Historic Green Springs, Inc., Gordonsville, Virginia.

Smoked Barbecued Pork Shoulder adapted from *The Huntsville Heritage Cookbook*, compiled by The Grace Club Auxiliary, Inc., ©1967. By permission of The Grace Club Auxiliary, Huntsville, Alabama.

Snow-Frosted Ham adapted from *Buckner Heritage Cookbook*, compiled and edited by Buckner Heritage Cookbook Committee, ©1978. By permission of Buckner Baptist Benevolences, Dallas, Texas.

Stuffed Pork Chops courtesy of Mrs. Roger Waller, Birmingham, Alabama.

Sykes Inn Smithfield Ham adapted from *Virginia Cookery, Past and Present* by The Women's Auxiliary of Olivet Episcopal Church, Franconia, Virginia.

Texas Basting Sauce by Maureen Mooney Jenkins, Austin, first appeared in *Cook 'em Horns* by The Ex-Students' Association of the University of Texas, Austin, ©1981. By permission of The Ex-Students' Association.

Text and graphics for "Good to Know" chapter adapted from information supplied by the National Live Stock and Meat Board, Chicago, Illinois.

Text, page 54, adapted from Duncan Hines' *Food Odessey*, published by Thomas Y. Crowell, ©1955. By permission of Harper and Row, New York.

Text, page 71, adapted from *Eating, Drinking, and Visiting in the South, an Informal History* by Joe Gray Taylor, ©1982. By permission of Louisiana State University Press, Baton Rouge, Louisiana.

Text, page 107, adapted from *Mrs. Blackwell's Heart of Texas Cookbook* by Louise B. Dillow and Deenie B. Carver. By permission of Corona Publishing Company, San Antonio, Texas.

W.W. Seals Barbecue Tips adapted from *Helen Exum's Cookbook*, ©1982. By permission of Helen McDonald Exum, Chattanooga, Tennessee.

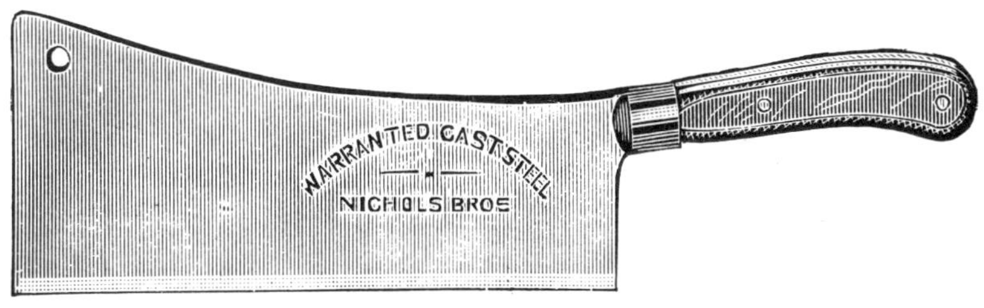

INDEX